Eager Traveller

An environmentally friendly book printed and bound in England by
www.printondemand-worldwide.com

Mixed Sources
Product group from well-managed
forests, and other controlled sources
www.fsc.org Cert no. TT-COC-002641
© 1996 Forest Stewardship Council
FSC

PEFC
PEFC/16-33-415

PEFC Certified
This product is
from sustainably
managed forests
and controlled
sources
www.pefc.org

This book is made entirely of chain-of-custody materials

www.fast-print.net/store.php

EAGER TRAVELLER

Copyright © Joanna Quant-Saunders 1990

A catalogue record for this book is available from the British Library

ISBN 978-178456-048-5

First published 1990
Second edition published 2014 by
FASTPRINT PUBLISHING
Peterborough, England.

EAGER TRAVELLER

by

Joanna Quant Saunders

Happy Reading

J Quant Saunders

Dedicated to
The First Two - Elizabeth and Janet
The Big Five - Martin, Teresa, Barry, Barb and Deanna
The Small Three - Lesley, Sarah and Sam
and the wider family who waited so long to read it

CONTENTS

Chapter One

Like Sir John Betjeman, I love St Pancras station, and when very young it was my favourite and most exciting place. I found that great adventures began and ended there. The sheer size of the place filled me with amazement, and the fact that my white gloves immediately became a delicate shade of dove grey on entering that vast cathedral-like building only added extra interest. Words of warning like, "Don't touch anything," rose unheeded into the cavernous roof space along with clouds of steam hissing like all the snakes in creation, with clangs and bangs and smells of sulphur and soot which seemed the necessary ingredients for Dante's Inferno. Years ago, it was fashionable to denigrate that Victorian edifice and I am glad the poet came to its defence.

We always left London at Christmas, *en route* for Burton-on-Trent, to stay with my Grandma and Grandad Renwick who lived on the Branston Road. The cottage in which they lived was very small, consisting of two tiny rooms down and two, just as minute, upstairs, one of which was not strictly a bedroom at all, being only the space at the top of the stairs. To go up you stepped into a small cupboard in a corner of the kitchen and then discovered the stairs were circular; the space at the top was elevated to the status of bedroom by virtue of the fact that my dad's youngest brother, Ern, had to sleep somewhere, and it seemed to be a matter for congratulation that he managed to get all six foot three of himself into the room at all.

The parlour was typically North country with the front door opening directly off the street and was used only on Sundays, funerals and Coronation days.

A blackleaded kitchen range stood in one corner, but the difference between this one and the everyday one in the kitchen was the ornateness of its design. The oven door had scroll decoration, brass handles and hinges, finished off with a brass tap at one side where there was a boiler for hot water. In order to have the hot water in the first place, it all had to be carried through the house

9

in large jugs from the wash-house in the garden, and carried back for use in the same way.

The range boasted an enormous hook at the back of the chimney from which hung a sooty chain to support an iron cooking pot or kettle.

There were a number of hooks in the ceiling beams from which large chunks of home cured bacon dangled, and I had made many visits before I realised that when my dad said, "Good God mother, you've got some good pictures up," he was not alluding to The *Monarch of the Glen* or to *Dignity and Imprudence,* but to the bacon.

The furniture was all Victorian horsehair and mahogany and wherever there was a shelf it had a green velvet drop with bobbles on it, fastened along the front edge. Many shelves were needed because Grandad Renwick was a taxidermist in his spare time, and several examples of his artistry were on display. Two ends were thus served; should a prospective client arrive to talk about a commission the items on display could be used as a guide for further work, or when he was sitting in his armchair, grandad could contemplate his past achievements.

My favourite was a large badger whose teeth appeared to have been borrowed from a lion and I was glad it was behind glass. In a bigger case was a beautiful fox in a stalking posture, ears pricked and one paw raised. Presenting his rump to Reynard, a prime cock pheasant with glistening plumage, head slightly turned, looking alert but not unduly troubled, was about to step forward. I always felt that if I were to blink the scene would change in an instant and Reynard would be going back the way he came with the pheasant slung over his shoulder.

A smaller case held several small birds indiginous to the English countryside. Some were in the act of pecking, others were perched on twigs and one of these was in full song, according to its beak and the small bulge at the throat.

I wish now that I had understood what an artist that man was. All the cases had suitable backgrounds for the subjects, with stones, wheatears, barley, dried grasses and twigs, even snail shells under a leaf. How sad that one so gifted should have drunk his substance away so early, condemning his Mary Anne to a life of sadness and hardship.

I paid more frequent visits after my grandad died as granny

was glad of some company, and in any case my life was not very lively in London, although there was a stream of uncles, aunts and spouses coming and going who sometimes took me on little jaunts if father approved.

When staying alone at Branston I slept with my gran in the big double bed with its feather mattress so soft you could fancy you were falling into a cloud.

Such fanciful notions were quickly dispelled when my gran in her voluminous nightdress climbed into bed and said, as she did every night, "Eh lass, thank God for a good bed." She must have had mixed feelings about that bed, thinking of it now. Her children were conceived and born in it, illnesses and accidents nursed in it and some had died and were laid out in it. As was my grandad, for all the neighbours to stand by his body and pay their last respects, making remarks like, "Eh, you were a good wife to 'im Mary Ann", or "He's not a bad cooler, m'wench."

Mary Ann must have been thankful that the chapter had come to an end. She had had a hard life with a job at the local brewery, her large family, and she took in washing in her spare time, while her handsome husband was running swiftly through the inheritence left him by his father who had been in business as a patten maker and was a smallholder.

There were all kinds of interesting things for a lonely child to do at 40 Branston Road. I made a daily tour of the neighbours' gardens and pigsties, for at this time every cottage had a pig to be killed for home consumption and I went to the farm every morning for the milk fresh from the cow and still warm.

Tom Laxton, the man who first employed my father, lived near by; he was one of my regulars; he kept terriers for show, and for ratting, had two pigs down his garden and had a daughter two years older than myself who let me play with her dolls in the event of there being nothing better to do.

I enjoyed all of this, but the highlight of the visit, was to mount the wooden box at the foot of the garden wall and drop down to the other side on to the Oxhay. This was a collection of water meadows through which the River Trent made its serene progress. The sight of a few bullocks grazing on the lush green grass to fatten for market caused decisions to be made and remade. Whether to walk further and only nip back to the shelter of the wall if the creatures raised their heads, or should we go in the opposite direction away from the danger? In the end I always put a brave face on it, at the same time ensuring that someone else was between me and the mobile Sunday dinners.

When we went into town for shopping the only thing I ever saw were the railway lines crossing every street connecting brewery property on both sides of the road, and I got a great excitement out of seeing the engines so close when the level crossing gates were across the roadway to let the wagons pass from one yard to another.

While the grown-ups chatted I watched the gangs unloading and loading the wagons, and the beer barrels always seemed too big for those who had to hump them, and the man who had to lick the pencil and did the scribbling was invariably the largest and bulkiest specimen in sight.

We always had a disjointed walk into town, every one knew my gran and my dad and I was known as 'Charley's girl' so I was asked a dozen times how I was getting on at school, and how old I was, and hadn't I grown. When they spoke to my dad there was an element of 'local boy makes good in the big city' in the conversation, a slight envy on the part of the locals, and a great tendency on father's part to gild the lily.

If I went out with 'Young Ern' that was a plus; none of dad's folk were as strict as my dad and I always had the feeling of being 'let out'. We had snowball fights or messed about by the river and always arrived back at 40 Branston Road covered in mud or wet through; Ern always got ticked off for "Letting her get in that state. What will our Charl say?" but it never seemed important when Ern, with a sly wink put a record on his portable gramophone and we sang together the hit of the day *Eat More Fruit*.

We had no such fripperies at our house as portable gramophones and although times were changing fast around us my dad was still in the 'Victoria and Dear Albert' era.

He believed that the best way to spur people on was to denigrate everything they did, but as we now know, this only knocks the stuffing out of them and makes them introverted. Perhaps his attitude contributed to my consuming desire to travel, known in the family as my 'Itchy feet'. It may also have been an unconcious desire on my part to put as great a distance as possible between him and me.

Whenever I went away from home my violin went in order that I could keep up my practise and thinking back my heart goes out to long suffering relatives on both sides of the family who were forced to sit through hours of Handel's *Largo*, the *Merry Peasant, March of the Hussars* and *Wedgewood Blue* followed by *Bluebells of Scotland* and any music-hall hit dad could think of at the time.

Miss Palk, my music teacher, had said, "never play by ear," but she had not reckoned with my dad. I had a good ear and a facility for picking up a tune, and in any case I was usually so desperate to do what father said and not rock the boat, that I got things right pretty quickly; however, I had a sort of built-in defence mechanism which came into play if dad kept me at it for too long. This would be triggered off by a wrong note which would bring odium down on my head, which would add to my considerable misery from standing in the centre of the room, playing before so many people, and the consequence was that I began to fiddle faster and faster, eventually leaving dad's voice trailing behind. When realisation came my hair would stick to my forehead and I knew a rocket would shortly be coming my way.

These visits occasionally coincided with a Dog Show and mum and I would go to help prepare the entries for the ring. Dad had been breeding terriers of one kind or another since leaving the army in 1918 and was starting to have some success. He liked to let his home town see he was still about, although he lived and earned his living in the capital. He would tell me to take one of the dogs into the show ring, which I generally liked to do, until the inevitable moment when I did, or omitted to do something that father thought I should or should not have done, in which case he would bellow instructions from his place in the line-up, or from the ringside. More often than not tears resulted, but every cloud has a silver lining and sometimes I got a prize, though not the one the dog had been entered for. A box of chocolates from Baroness Burton did much to alleviate my wounded spirit.

By the age of ten I was travelling to Burton alone, my mum putting me on the train at St. Pancras, having first asked one of the ladies in the carriage if she would be kind enough to see that I got out at the right station.

Mum would then exhort me to, "be a good girl and do what grandma tells you," then with a quick kiss she would be out on the platform as the guard blew his whistle and we were off. Leaving home was never one of my worries for away from dad I was free as air and there was always so much to see and wonder at that time seemed immaterial and non-existant.

Why, I wondered, did the enormous chimneys at London Brick not topple over and why were three of them innocent of smoke when the rest of them had smoke going up for miles it seemed, before the plumes bent sideways and lost their murky substance in the grey skies?

Leaving Leicester, feeling not quite the thing between the nice lady's sweets, the motion of the train and the general excitement, I told myself we were nearly there and averted disaster by diving into the toilet clutching the large white handkerchief without which I never travelled.

At that time trains had no corridors, but each compartment had its own toilet in the centre of the row of seats allowing room for two seats either side of the toilet door and five or six seats facing them.

They were always clean and well appointed, with linen towels for the use of the passengers and soap in the basin. At one stage steel basins were in vogue; these could be fastened back on to the wall after use and I would spend a good ten minutes viewing my distorted features in the concave underside of the basin.

After the introduction of corridor trains waiters in black trousers and white monkey-jackets provided a full service and chefs cooked on the way.

I loved to pop out into the corridor and savour the cloud of expensive perfume and cigar smoke left on the air by the elegantly dressed first-class passengers going along for lunch or afternoon tea. Even today a whiff of "Coty" or cigar aroma can transport me immediately to the Olympia, the old White City and the International Horse show, when only the upper crust went to such events, all in full evening rig and the ladies sporting furs and jewels.

No jeans or cowboy boots, nor spiky green hair, and no graffiti in the toilets, but sadly, outside there were kids with the behinds out of their britches and the soles of their boots parting company with the uppers. Who shall say "Those were the days?"

A few miles from Burton brewing smells were on the air and I was glad to be nearing my destination and my uncle who would be there to meet me. The kind lady reminded me to put a comb through my hair and said how pleased she was that I had been a good girl. On one occasion a lady retied my hair ribbon and came down onto the platform to tell my uncle that "Her mother need never worry about her wherever she goes."

I suppose I walked out of the station wearing a very smug expression as I was seldom praised for anything. My dad never believed in it.

My uncle had been a Grenadier Guardsman and we used to go down to see him on duty at the Palace. I was well briefed not to call out as we walked past, and felt very puffed up about it all, but sorry he could not do mounted duty as well in Whitehall. I really felt the king missed out by not having this paragon of virtue permanently on guard. Who could tell then, that he would make such a mess of his life that he felt the only way to clear it up was to end it all which he did when I was fifteen. I was a loser too, as he would have been one of my champions against outrageous fortune.

My itchy feet had been given a lot of encouragement over the years from the beginning. Both my parents had enjoyed travelling in their respective jobs, she as a housekeeper and he as a stud groom to some of the highest families in the land. They had infact met while working at the same place in 1909. When they each left 'to better' themselves, as the saying goes, they continued to correspond but seldom met. In 1914 Charlie joined up and was soon off to France. Alice continued to write to him and when he came back to Blighty in early 1918 everyone took it for granted that they would marry. So Alice drifted into marriage and shortly after wished she could drift out again.

She found he was very keen on money, of which she saw very little, and there was no pleasing him on any level, but being the woman she was she stuck to her bargain and was not released from her bondage for forty-two years.

My arrival was the absolute end; he was so sure the baby was to be a boy but being confronted by a female was more than he could bear and he felt fate had played him a dirty trick. To top it all there was to be no second chance as it was impossible for Alice to have another child; from then on he showed little affection for either of us, merely doing his duty in the way of food and clothing and surprisingly as it appears now, I was always sent either to his family or to mum's sister, Amy, for the summer holidays.

Dad's sister, Nell, had married Alec and was living in Derby and I spent so much time there that I began to feel as much at home as in London. My Uncle Alec became my great friend and in after years when my two daughters, Be and Janet were small we used to go in great family parties to many of the beauty spots around Derby.

Matlock was a favourite place for all of us and we never tired of the Roman mines where every fifth person in line was given a lantern to light the way. Thorpe Cloud was a great place for us where the young ones could climb the slopes and cross the river on stepping-stones.

Chapter Two

The holidays at Lymington were quite different; to start with the journey was much prettier. According to the time of year there were primroses and cowslips growing beside the line and in the late spring the embankments were obscured by masses of rhododendron bushes whose flowers ranged in different colours from palest pink to strong red. They were a magnificent sight and my nose was glued to the window for much of the way.

Mum's sister, Amy, had married her George, who was head-gardener on a big estate. They lived in a pretty cottage that went with the job, and all mum's family went back and forth at a great rate. The family in the 'big house' were known as 'the people' and if 'the people' were away or abroad at the time of any family visits the chauffeur would meet the train at Lymington Town with the Rolls and we would purr through the countryside feeling very satisfied with things. However, should 'the people' be in residence, my Uncle George would meet the train with the pony and trap, which was also a great thrill, and I would have been hard put to it to have said which mode of transport was the greater pleasure.

There were seven under-gardeners, all vitally necessary to keep the estate in the manner to which it had become accustomed. Two tennis courts were kept in immaculate condition, and could be used by the staff in the absence of the family and there were several small specialist gardens within the whole. A rose garden, an Italian garden, a water garden with giant rhubarb-like leaves, iris, hostas and enormous buttercups growing in the water, an Alpine garden, a sunken garden with a fish pool and the immense walled kitchen garden, where peaches, nectarines, figs, apples, plums, greengages and pears grew around the mellow pink walls.

A great range of glasshouses produced out of season items, grapes, tomatoes, cucumbers, strawberries and melons, and on a decorative note there were dahlias, chrysanthemums and ferns.

I loved the fern house; it was slightly shaded, warm and damp and smelled of deep woods and violets. A great deal of heat was needed and much coke was burned through the year in order for these exotics to be enjoyed out of season. The coke would heat water which was then sent through pipes running around the greenhouses, and whoever was on duty went back to the garden at ten o'clock to stoke up the fire and check the temperatures in all the houses. Electric propagators were in the future, but happily, the seeds of my own interest in gardening were sown here, although I was not aware of it at the time.

Years after, during the war when flowers were in short supply, my Uncle George sent, by post, a small corsage of deep pink carnations and fern for me to wear at my wedding in 1940.

News came that the little cottage was to be demolished to make room for a larger house, in order that any visiting valets or chauffeurs could be accommodated more easily. Family holidays had to be adjusted for some months, but eventually my Grandfather Quant went down to inspect the new house, and soon there was a trail of family coming and going once again.

Everything about the new house was bang up-to-date and wonderful after the old place, without main sewerage or electricity, but the best place was the kitchen with its *pièce de résistance* in the far corner covered by a lid of polished wood. Hiding its glory from the casual observer it waited for Friday nights when it could be unveiled and filled with hot water from the coal-fired copper beside it.

When I was there on holiday there would sometimes be a variation of the routine and the Friday ritual had to be brought forward to Thursday, or Wednesday, or Tuesday even and on these occasions I was less than popular with my aunt, because every drop of water had to be carried from the tap at the sink to the copper to be heated and then carried from the copper to the bath. Luckily, there was a cold tap connected to the bath so things could have been worse, but not much.

The reason for all the commotion was my friend, Bruce. We went everywhere together, mostly on to the marsh, a large area of flat land composed mainly of sand dunes, rank grass and sea pinks growing in profusion, which hid a multitude of boggy places and was bound by the sea-wall.

We went out every day and the time inevitably came when there was nothing left to explore, and therefore no excuses for falling into the bogs.

This was the moment when Amy would wail, "Oh George, look at the state they're in. They'll have to go into the bath again."

Of course I was delighted. We had no such bath at home; ours was an old tin bath in front of the kitchen range and it doubled up on wash days for the family wash, so in the end it was yet another treat.

I had the water first while Bruce was banished to the garden until I had been dealt with. Then poor old Bruce would be hauled in and given the treament, with my aunt muttering darkly "Thank Heavens her father didn't see her," or "You bad dog, get you two together for five minutes and you're in trouble!"

Bruce, looking suitably penitent, would then be towelled off, and with my cocoa finished, we would trail across the hall and upstairs to the lavender-scented bedroom. A last look across the Solent at the lights of the Isle Of Wight, a last sniff at the aroma from below of the conifers after rain and I would be ready for bed, my hand dangling over the side so if I uncurled my fingers I could touch Bruce's head and get a swift lick before falling asleep.

In the normal way Bruce slept in his basket in the kitchen, but it was a special treat for both of us for him to sleep on the bedside rug. One bedtime I remember with great pleasure. I thought I heard faint music and got out of bed to look out of the window, and what a sight met my eyes. A lovely ocean-going liner, lit with fairy lights from stem to stern, sailing regally past with the the music from the dance band drifting beguilingly across the water. The next day my uncle told us it had been the *Empress of Britain* which I had seen before in her pristine white livery sailing into Southampton.

I believe the sight of that liner fuelled in me the urge to travel, but thirty years were to pass before I left these shores for the first time.

I had always been interested in things foreign and this may have been due to hearing my dad's experiences in the First World War. The names of battlefields and Northern French towns were as familiar to me as the street names in my part of London. Bethune, Arras, Ypres, the Marne, Verdun, Aix la Chappelle; if any of these names came into the conversation I held my breath and listened; Consequently I heard things descibed that prehaps I should not have heard.

I recall an advertisement for one of the animal charities which brought me to tears everytime I saw it. We saw it at all the horse shows and farm events for many years and it depicted a scene in

France of a sunken road with troops moving off after a battle. The road was filled with craters and a shell hole in the foreground contained a dead horse. A British Tommy was trudging away from the scene looking over his shoulder at his dead friend, and the caption underneath said, "Goodbye, old man."

Some of these places I have since visited and it is impossible to believe that the pleasant countryside was the place of such horror and carnage all those years ago, with evidence of how nature is repairing and renewing continously without any of us being aware of it.

In due course I managed to get a scholarship to the local polytechnic, and although I enjoyed it all , I did go through a period of misery wondering if I would be allowed to go on the school trip to Stratford on Avon. I had been in the Guides but dad had never agreed to my going to camp and I was prepared for refusal again.

Our form teacher was a formidible Scots lady who ruled us with a rod of iron disguised as a tongue. I especially noticed this one day when we had a housewifery lesson. During the period we had made jam, and another girl and I had been given the job of covering the jars and transferring them to the store cupboard.We did a neat task and the jars stood in rows on the top shelf like soldiers on parade all the labels facing the front, and we agreed that 'Old Nick' would be pleased with us.

We had been talking and laughing during the work and as I came down the step-ladder giving one last look at the jars I realised that I had popped every one of the cellophane covers.

Why I had this mental aberration I will never know. I remembered doing it in a far off sort of way as if I were seeing someone else doing it, but it was I who had the lines to do. "I must not pop jam covers" five hundred times which meant staying in after school every day for a week. I shall never forget 'Old Nick's' face as the enormity of what I had done sank into her consiousness; expressions chased across her countenance in swift succession from sheer disbelief to bewilderment to fury, giving way to sadness that one of her "best girls" could have such a streak of "absolute vandalism," and all I could do was stand mute and agree with every word.

Come time, all was forgiven and as I had paid strict attention to my duties at home, exercising six dogs before and after school each day, feeding and cleaning out, I managed to stay on the right side of father, and eventually found myself on the train with Miss Nicholson and the rest of the girls.

The earlier magic of going somewhere had never faded and while some of the girls had not been on a train before and sat hunched in their seats awaiting the time to get off, I studied the countryside as always. I loved the little brooks that meandered across the meadows in a series of S bends with willows and brambles on their banks, and the dairy herds streaming through a gate to pasture, or a bunch of bullocks standing around a galvanised water trough.

" 'Ow jer know all this about farms an' 'orses an' animals an' stuff?" one of the girls asked, and I was pleased to tell them that my dad and his family came from Staffordshire and were from farming stock and that although my mum was a Londoner born, all her family were 'down along Devon' folk.

"Cor, you ain' 'arf lucky goin' about like yer do," said one, to which I replied, "Yes, but you can go out if you want, and you can go to the pictures, and you get spends, and you don't have to take the dogs for a walk before and after school, do you?"

"My mum would tell the ol' man to do it 'is self," said another girl, but as far as I was concerned these remarks applied to people who lived on a completely different planet from me, and as we were rapidly approaching the station we gathered our stuff up and prepared to leave the train.

A charabanc awaited our arrival and a short drive brought us to Stratford where a chorus of "oohs" and "aahs" greeted the sight of the river with its resident swans and cygnets.

We had recently read *Romeo and Juliet* and plans were in hand for us to put on *Much Ado About Nothing,* in our last year and this was the reason for our interest in the Bard's home town, but I forgot him when I saw the old half timbered buildings. The narrow streets and the leaning houses were a new departure for me. Although I had seen plenty of pictures, I had never been close enough to see the adze and axe marks from centuries earlier and I was astounded and filled with amazement.

In the birthplace I began to see that trees had been cut into slices for the floor boards, and there was the smell of the polish of hundreds of years. I knew about beeswax and turpentine from my mum who had told me that the making of polish and candles had been part of the duties of the under housemaid in large houses.

Long before I was ready to leave, we were whisked off to Anne

21

Hathaway's cottage, where I got just as carried away as previously, when we heard about Shakespeare's will, his second-best bed and his brush with the law when he poached Sir Thomas Lucy's venison. Getting his own back, the Bard, they say, penned these lines;

A parliamentary member, a justice of peace
At home a poor scarecrow, in London an asse.
If Lowsie is Lucy as some folk miscalle it
Then Lucy is Lowsie whatever befall it

I can imagine all the apprentice boys in the City cat-calling the great man as he went about his affairs in the Capital.

On this whirlwind trip we also saw Guy's Cliffe Mill and standing by the water we heard of Guy's adventures.

He began his career as a page in Warwick Castle and fell for the earl's daughter, Felice, and in order to prove his love for his lady he travelled across Europe and into Turkey where he fought the Saracens. His prowess made him the most famous fighting man of his time, and on his return married his Felice. Before long the earl died and Guy found he had succeeded to the title. In gratitude to God, who had given him so much in life, Guy set off for the Holy Land to have another shot at the Saracens, which says little for his gratitude to Felice, who spent many years alone, only catching up with her errant spouse two weeks before his death in the nearby cave where he had spent the last year or two. He died in his wife's arms, and consumed with grief, poor Felice jumped into the Avon and was drowned.

As we returned to the station we had a short visit to Warwick Castle in its beautiful setting, mirrored on the quietly flowing waters of the Avon. We loved the peacocks and had a quick look into the dungeon which gave us the shudders, and we were glad to get back to the train.

When our essays were handed in mine had no Shakespeare dates and facts, I had waffled on about the town's buildings. In due course we put on *Much Ado About Nothing*, which was a success I'm happy to say. I played Don John, chief scoundrel (who bled if pricked) and I overheard our drama teacher telling someone she thought we had derived a great deal of benefit from the school trip.

Chapter Three

Although I still visited Burton, Derby and Lymington, my next new journey came after I started work. Father insisted, to my mother's horror that I was to go into service, and after an application to the famous servants agency in Derby, I began work in Piccadilly as a scullery maid. The work was not a problem as everything done in my home had met the standards to which my mother had been trained in her time, but to say I hated every minute is an understatement.

Being the newest recruit I had orders from everyone, from the housekeeper, the head-kitchen maid, the second and third kitchen maids, the still-room maid and even the odd man who spent a lot of his time in the scullery stoking his boilers but his orders were of the, "what about a cup of tea, Joanie?" variety. These were only the kitchen staff. In addition there was a head housemaid and three lesser housemaids, the butler and two footmen, a lady's maid, who only appeared for meals in the housekeeper's room, and when the grandchildren of the family arrived we then had a nanny, a nursemaid and a schoolroom maid as well, all of whom truly believed they were much more important than anyone else.

The whole set up was a living illustration of the old entry in an autograph book; "Big fleas have little fleas upon their backs to bite 'em, And little fleas have smaller fleas, and so on ad infinitum." And this was the case that servants had servants, who had servants.

I knew I would have to grin and bear it for at least a year in order to get a reference, without which a job could not be obtained, but I must say that life was not all doom and gloom and we lower orders had a lot of fun along the way. In any case I was looking forward to the day when the house was closed and we would all be going to the country houses, one at Newmarket for the races and the other at North Berwick for the golf.

Cecil Lodge was a large house with a large outside staff of gardeners and laundry maids none of whom we ever saw. Newmarket itself was quite interesting for us because sometimes we finished work in time to see a race or two, but in general we had no proper time off while we were away, but had extra time out in London to compensate, which suited me and one other girl as we had our homes there.

Several of our staff would put money on a horse having a connection with the family, but with me getting eight shillings a week plus two shillings laundry money and two shillings beer money, I was very unlikely to use it for betting. I spent all I had left on books after putting four shillings in the post office, which in a way was a pointer to my craze to travel. I bought the *Wide World* magazine, the *Geographical Magazine, Lilliput* and *Picture Post*. Even my favourite hymn *From Greenland's Icy Mountains* was a giveaway.

I loved the horsy-atmosphere which was to be expected as dad worked with them all his life, and sometimes we saw the strings exercising on the downs. On one of the odd occasions when we were able to go out in the afternoon I stood at the rail with the punters shouting "come on Steve" as he won the one thousand guineas on Exhibitionist.

We all worked hard during the week and looked forward to the Saturday night hop in the town, never getting there before ten o'clock, only to be disappointed at the lack of anything that was in any way, tall, dark and handsome.

We youngsters had forgotten that in a racing community all the young fellows were aspiring jockeys or even ex-jockeys and stable-lads, and in most cases we could have put them under our arm and forgotten about them, so we all went off that idea until we got to Scotland. Of course, we still enjoyed the dressing up with our long dresses, silver shoes and bags. Around that time most people were wearing marina green and marina pink, favoured by the Greek princess who was to marry into our royal family.

The exodus to Scotland was an experience. First signs of the forthcoming departure were the great number of tea chests brought into the kitchen. All the copper saucepans were cleaned with silver sand and vinegar or lemons left over from the cooking, an operation which had far reaching effects, because every winter since then the cracks caused in my fingers open and bleed again. Some pans would need to be retinned and were sent off to be dealt with and sent on to the Scottish address. Seven sizes of pans, fish kettles, Banburys (bain-maries), preserving pans, bombe moulds, jelly moulds, tea kettles, stock pots, frying and omlette pans, all of copper, were packed and stacked to await collection by L.M.S. or L.N.E.R.

We all had sleepers to Scotland and the luxury of an early morning call when the steward brought a tea-tray. Early call was right; we were all standing on the platform of a small station waiting for the local train at five-thirty a.m. when Joan made history again. In the thin morning air, hugging ourselves into our coats, too tired or too miserable to talk, and suddenly my alarm clock went off. Its true, it was inside my case but in the silence it was like a fire alarm and although nothing was said to me directly I could see the housekeeper muttering darkly to the head kitchen maid, and I knew I would be called upon to pay the bill some time.

Again we had little time off. The house was full of golfing lunatics with their valets, ladies' maids, chauffeurs and poor relations. Early rising was a necessary part of life, otherwise nothing would have got done; the kitchen at seven in the morning was like rush hour at a main line station. Morning trays were laid and stacked ready the night before, leaving the tea to be made and the appropriate thin bread and butter, biscuits or fairy toast to be placed on the correct trays. It all sounds straightforward, but the whole operation was like a giant jigsaw puzzle; some had tea with no sugar, some tea with no milk and they all required different teas. Some brought their own mixture which was labelled and left in the kitchen. Others demanded Assam, China, Orange Pekoe, Soochong, black or green- the most demanding of all were the valets and ladies' maids who were aping their employers.

At seven-thirty the butler was directing his footmen, which tray went to which bedroom. Valets and maids, who had received their calls earlier, were adding to the melee, demanding the tray for their master or mistress and expecting exclusive attention. Then by eight-fifteen, as though a switch had been thrown, unbelievable quiet had descended upon the kitchen and its staff. Time for a quick cup of tea and we were up to our necks in breakfast. We were all cogs in a well oiled machine and in most cases things went without a hitch.

We underlings took it in turn to have an hour off some afternoons and as we all had bikes we were able to see a little of the locality. We went up the Berwick Law a few times, and reading about it afterwards I discovered it had been witch and wizard country in the old times. A coven of two hundred was recorded as being concerned in a plot against King James VI of Scotland at the time of his marriage to Princess Anne of Denmark.

Bass Rock was a feature of the North Berwick seascape, a bird sanctuary for many years, and earlier a prison some two miles out in the Firth of Forth, a gaunt black rock rising vertically out of the sea, from which escape would appear impossible. In 1691 some Jacobites were in the fortress as prisoners, and instead of escaping, they drove away the guards and held the rock for two years in defiance of the English forces.

The house where we lived was called 'Westerdunes' and was situated on the coast road a little way out of town. The golf course was between us and the sea, but we could often go for a stroll on the shore, between finishing at two-thirty and starting to get the drawing-room tea ready at three-thirty. One day I had permission to ride into town to the post office and I dallied overlong. Consequently I came back as though the Devil himself was behind me and as I turned into the drive I met her ladyship turning out.

We met noisily and her ladyship, being French, added to the din, but we parted swiftly. The Rolls travelled across the road coming gently to rest in the hedge, while I took to the air, executing a delicate arc through the atmosphere landing with a thump on the gravel drive. I had only grazes and a cut arm, the scar I carry still, but after her ladyship had visited the kitchen and expressed her opinion of lunatic cyclists I was in less than good odour, but the Rolls was undamaged save for a thick film of dust thrown up by the skid.

We discovered the house was haunted, but we were not unduly troubled by the knowledge. Our room was on the top floor and we all knew that ghosts haunted after midnight, so going up to bed presented no problem, provided that we went to up well before the witching hour; however if we had been working late we waited for each other and ascended in a posse; none of us ever saw or heard anything untoward but one morning we heard the head servants discussing an event the previous night.

Frederick, our first footman, had a bedroom beside the back door next to the strong-room in which the silver was kept. The day had been hectic and we were all very late in getting to bed and he was last of all. Putting the remaining items in the strong-room, he heard steps outside in the stone passage. He expected to see the butler or one of the other footmen, but there was no one about. Thinking himself mistaken, he finished his duties, locked up and retired for the night. Half undressed he again heard footsteps, so he called out and opened his door and again the passage was empty; now he began to think and also to listen, and he was not disappointed. Shuffling footsteps as of feet in carpet slippers passed his door, and this time enough was enough, and he dashed through the house in his pyjamas calling to the two junior footmen to let him in, and he spent a disturbed night with them. The rules were changed at once, a room was found for him upstairs and locking the strong-room became the last duty of the butler before turning in.

After several weeks in Scotland we were told a trip to Edinburgh was imminent. Under-servants were to go first and upper-servants the following week. In the event we went in style in the Rolls and amused ourselves by waving in the manner of Queen Mary and even James joined in the general hilarity and behaved with exaggerated servility.

We were five in our batch, our duties being covered by those left behind. Millie, the head kitchen-maid, myself now the second kitchen-maid, the new scullery-maid, Olive, a second housemaid, whose name I forget and another house maid called Sybil, but who was known as Connie, because her ladyship's daughter-in-law's name was Sybil and it was unthinkable to have a servant using the name of one of the family.

When I first arrived at the job someone said my name would have to be changed as the other son's wife was Joan, and I was incensed; I thought it was a damned cheek and was quite ready to say so, but nothing came of it as none of my duties took me 'through the front', and no muddle could arise.

Arriving in Princes Street, James, set us down, straight faced now, telling us to be there at exactly the right time for going back; the Rolls purred away and we set off to see the sights. We decided to see the castle first and puffed our way up the Mound. I must say, having always been nutty about history I was the only one thrilled to bits. The view from the ramparts over the city, the Grecian Columns on Calton Hill, the one o'clock gun, Scott's monument, the Scottish War Memorial, the Garrison Pets' Cemetery and another look across the city in case I missed anything the first time. I had a great time, but the others were tired and bored long before I had had my fill.

I felt guilty that the girls might be fed up with me, so I thought I would do without question what they wished, which was to go to the shops. We set off across the cobbles and through the several gateways over the moat and out onto the esplanade.

Beyond Earl Haig's statue was the cab rank, but something unbelievable took our eye. Standing between two taxis was a horse drawn vehicle, now but a shadow of its former glory. Once it had been handsome, a black glossy coachwork picked out in gold with a folding hood and soft leather buttoned seats. The driver, a small man, dressed in black, wearing a bowler hat, sat in the driving seat, head forward, shoulders hunched and looking the picture of misery, as did his dejected looking horse hanging in the shafts. The whole ensemble seemed to be covered in a fine green mould as though it had been kept in a damp cellar for years.

As we approached this relic the taxi in front accepted a fare and moved away, and the driver stirred himself to edge his equipage into the space vacated by the taxi.

We had a little chat to see if we could decide whether this apparition was a taxi or not. Millie being senior to the rest assumed the position of spokesman and asked the question. "Aye, I am." was the reply in strong brogue. The dialect flummoxed Millie a bit and she hesitated; our hero said, "D'ye no' wish tae gae doon tae the palace, lassies?"

Olive asked, "How much will it cost?" Millie turned again to the driver and he muttered something none of us could catch. We tried again and found that "twa and saxpence" would cover the cost of the ride, so in we got, five of us in four seats and we were more than satisfied with our situation. To the sound of hooves on the cobbles our driver began to talk about the Royal Mile.

Unfortunately his accent was so broad that none of us really understood much, and between castle and palace the only words I caught were "Knox's House," "milk" and "Mary's Bath". Arriving at the Palace of Holyrood we produced the fare, thanked him very much, and turned into the imposing iron gates as he called, "Guid day t'ye lassies."

Having read of poor Mary, Queen of Scotts, I found the ancient pile most interesting, but with time so limited we scooted round and then tore up the Royal Mile in search of afternoon tea. This we found at one of Crawford's tea shops in Princes Street. We did justice to scones and jam and a large pot of best Ceylon, and sailed forth to deal with the presents to take home for those poor souls in our families who were not blest with opportunities to visit 'foreign' parts.

We came out with everything imaginable covered in tartan silk.

Silver mounted grouse claws, Celtic pendants, socks in Argyle check as favoured by H.R.H. the Prince of Wales, and a trumps indicator in Black Watch tartan for my dad who was a whist maniac.

Suddenly our lovely free day was over, and we hurried to our rendezvous with James who waited with the Rolls, and as we purred away I vowed I would be back to really see that fascinating city. Forty-five years were to elapse before I set foot in Edinburgh, and the same feeling of excitement consumed me as when I was sixteen. In fact there is such a 'thing' between me and Edinburgh that I really think I must have lived there in a previous life.

The weather became very bad and our great barn of a bedroom was like an ice house, so we decided something had to be done about it. There was a large fire place in the middle of one wall, so we rearranged the beds so as to have a clear space before the hearth, and the next morning I mentioned the refrigerator we slept in to the housekeeper.

"No good telling me that my girl," she said, "You won't be able to have a fire up there. Besides, you don't get time to sit up there. When you go up it's time to get into bed."

We all felt a bit huffy about this and a lot of talk went on and finally we came to the conclusion that even the dogs had a warm place to sleep; we would have our fire, and not mention it, on the basis that what they didn't know wouldn't worry them. The difficulty was in getting the necessary ingredients upstairs, and more cloak and dagger stuff took place than in a Douglas Fairbanks picture.

Accordingly we all made extra trips up to the room during the day, each time smuggling a few bits of coal or kindling, and soon we had a cardboard box full of coal and a smaller one full of firewood, and the odd man had been heard to say about the housemaids, "Those bloody girls must be eating this chopping wood."

That night the first one up to to bed lit the fire, and by the arrival of the last one up, there was a lovely warm space to sit in, on our hard chairs. We could foresee a happy and comfortable time ahead, with a box of chocolates or a bag of toffees being passed around. The only fly in our ointment was the fact that a cup of tea could not be made up there.

We decided to work on the tea as our next project, but before our plans were formulated Nemesis struck, the balloon went up and all hell was let loose.

I was in the kitchen one evening putting her ladyship's spinach through the seive when her maid appeared in the doorway looking very agitated and slightly dishevelled; her face was red and slightly grubby as she glared at me and Millie and gasped, "You've done it now you stupid creatures. Her ladyship's gone mad and as soon as she's had another bath she will be down here to give you notice."

"Notice?" we said together. "Why?" We thought of all the things we had done for which we could expect to be given notice, but long before we were on the track she shouted, "You'll soon see my girls," and taking the cook by the elbow, the woman launched into a lengthy tale and as we listened the hair on our scalps began to rise.

It appeared that her ladyship, having had her bath was standing before the fireplace wearing her bathrobe and trying to decide what to wear down to dinner, when an enormous cloud of soot descended into the fire. Rooted to the spot the poor woman got blacker by the second, as did the dinner dress under discussion, and the Aubusson carpet on which she stood. Miss Ross who had been further away and had quicker reflexes than her irate employer, had missed the worst, becoming only sightly tarnished as she helped her ladyship away from the disaster area and into the bathroom.

The odd man was sent for to explain why the chimney had not been swept a few days before and never having taken part in an interview through a bathroom door before, his answers were almost incomprehensible, but managed to suggest that other chimneys ran into the one concerned and should he go up and take a look? He did so and discovered that we'd been having a fire in our room, which explained everything and he lost no time in getting himself off the hook and we girls on it.

Long lectures were the order of the day, and after the clean up, her ladyship had another go and after that, the cook and the butler were waiting in the wings to say their piece. The "effrontery of servants today" was the topic at the dinner table that night, and again at breakfast, with family and guests giving their opinions on what should be our fate, only stopping short of "hang, draw and quarter".

Shortly after this we heard that the London house was being lent for a big society wedding, and although the event was to take place in the middle of our time in Scotland some staff were to travel back to London to help with the preparations, and to my delight I was one of those to go.

We young ones imagined we would all be travelling in a group, but instead I found myself *en route* in the sole company of the butler, and as he was in the top echelon I was well aware that decorum on my part had to be the order of the day.

As it turned out I found my companion to be an interesting conversationalist with a fund of ancedotes which kept me amused all the way. For the first time I lunched on a train and happily got the hang of coffee at speed without a spillage. The meal itself left me unimpressed, I had often had better at home, but the atmosphere was magical to me and the fact that I was waited on for a change went a long way to make up for being in the bottom slot for so long.

Having decided that a rarefied being like a butler is as human as the rest of us, I, as all Cinderellas before me, heard the clock strike twelve and hey presto, the following morning found me in uniform ready to do my bit for the big wedding.

What I recall most about this glittering social occasion was the slurp of champagne down the sink. The catering had been done by an outside firm and we saw to all the visiting staff, who were servants from the family homes of the happy couple.

Everything had been over ordered, especially the liquid refreshment, and anything not used came below stairs, including umpteen bottles of champagne started but not emptied, and who will drink champers with no fizz?

Late to bed that night and very tired, the cleaning up was done the next morning and all was made ready for a return north, those with families close enough had a couple of hours in which to see them, the others did shopping and the evening found us at King's Cross, ready for the 'off'.

There were some grumbles about the hours to be spent in the train, but as usual, I was just pleased to be going. Millie, Olive, Connie and I were all together taking turns at the washbasin and after a lot of giggling (and a knock on the wall from the next compartment) we settled about eleven o'clock. After our early call and tea-tray a mad scramble ensued to find our luggage which had not been placed in a good position for a quick getaway. By the skin of our teeth we fell out on the platform with the rest of our bleary-eyed party. As the express pulled away to continue its journey we had time to consider the day, as we waited to be ferried to North Berwick. It was cold and still dark, and we were glad to be rescued by the timely arrival of the Rolls, followed by the pony and trap for the luggage.

Unpacking in our freezing bedroom, I considered what some of the girls had been saying about better pay in temporary jobs, and I thought prehaps fairly soon I would move on to pastures new.

By now, having shared our working lives for several months, Millie and I had become good friends, a bond which lasted for many years. After I left I missed her lilting Welsh voice and the jokes we shared, not to mention the interest we each had in the other's young man. She was being courted by a tinsmith, and plans were in hand for a wedding in about two years. Housing was no problem in those days, as anyone who had a spare room would let it on a weekly basis, thereby supplementing a meager income, and Millie and Bob were going to start small and improve as they went along.

I was going out with the son of Dolly's employer, or I was when in London, and as he was a great letter writer a lot of nasty remarks came my way,

"He may write every day, but he could be anywhere," they said. Which was true. In fact I had a lot of post from uncles, aunts and cousins, as well as the weekly digest from mum and Dolly while I was away.

When golfing ceased the exodus took place in reverse. This time I travelled back with the cook and the scullery maid, leaving Millie and local help to clear up at that end, and she was to return to London with the butler and second footman while Frederick escorted us.

In days the dark old kitchen had been transformed to its former splendour with no indication that it had been deserted for so long. The steel rails were burnished brightly and the copper pans and all the other paraphernalia had been cleaned and hung in its place; paint had been washed and all was shipshape and Bristol fashion.

Our time off was restored us, doubled in fact, to make up for our loss while away. Millie came home if we were off together, which we seldom were, and these visits compensated in part for her home being so far away, and mum, having been in that position herself during her working life, was pleased to take her in; our friendship lasted many years and after my own marriage we met each time I came home when mum would let her know and Millie would come for tea.

My elder daughter was born in 1942 and this gave Millie and Bob a lot of pleasure as there were no children for them, after several years of marriage, but perhaps fate knew better than we; pre-war Croydon was eliminated from the face of the earth by the Luftwaffe, and from then 'till now there has been no word of them.

Chapter Four

When the year I had given myself was up, I placed my name on the agency books again and several jobs were offered. I quite fancied one as a kitchen maid in the High Commision in Canada and promptly applied for it. I was told that I was too young and I finally tried for a place in Princes Gate. Attending the interview, I found that the hunting season was spent in Leicestershire, Quorn country in fact, and as I had heard my dad speak of this part of the country many times, I felt that I knew it already. He had been a hunt servant, stud groom, whipper-in and head groom, having come up from the bottom, holding the horse's head while the local vet climbed in and out of his trap.

I was accepted and soon found myself in new surroundings in Old Woodhouse. The house was called "Beau Manor" and it truely was a beautiful house. All the timber had been grown on the estate hundreds of years before, and the carvings were wonderful. The hall from which the stairs rose to the galleries, was enormous, and was the scene of the staff party at Christmas, when, like Saturnalia, all roles were reversed. The lady of the house began the dancing with the butler, followed by the master with the housekeeper; this procedure was followed all down the heirachy, with the most junior staff member partnering the similar family sprig. When the niceties had been observed, we all danced with whoever asked us. I had a turn with the youngest son but I had no idea I was dancing with an Admiral-to-be.

Beau Manor, being an Elizabethan house, was built as three sides of a square with a courtyard in the centre, which made it an ideal setting for the meet. Although I abhorred the fox being torn to pieces at the end of his marathon, I always felt a surge in my blood at the sight of so much horseflesh, so many hounds, hunting pinks, black habits, side-saddles, top hats and our butler and footmen passing among the throng with the stirrup cup and lunch cake. We were allowed a few minutes to see the hunt move off and then it was back to work, because hunt days were extra busy. Stragglers would be returning to the house all through the day for many reasons; the horse may have gone lame, or could have thrown the rider, or they may have got lost and separated from the main body, or perhaps the rider just got tired. Whatever the reason we were cooking and preparing trays all day and would then have a dinner party for twenty or thirty at night.

Our time off was a half day each week and alternate Sundays. Well, not exactly off, as we were meant to go to church with the family and house guests. For several weeks after arriving at my new place I adhered to the rules, went to church and considered myself fortunate that I was not made to wear a bonnet. This had been the case in the old days, when each big house had its own style of bonnet, presumably in order for the vicar to denounce those who committed misdemeanours and be more easily identified.

During this time I was quite taken with our milk boy who delivered each day from the home farm; my previous heart-throb had been given his marching orders on my return from Scotland, when I discovered he had become one of Oswald Moseley's fascists. We had been reading reports of their activities in the press and I for one could not accept their habit of riding about in lorries through the East End of London throwing bricks through Jewish shop windows.

"Come and hear him speak," said my hero. "He is magnificent," he had not understood what I was talking about when I asked him what had Jews ever done to him. So that was the end of a beautiful friendship and we soon heard that one of his mates had achieved notoriety as "Lord Haw-Haw". The last I heard of the man was that he had driven his tank over the Rhine, so I hoped that his soul was eventually saved.

My new hero was Bernard, known to all as Bunny, a sporting lunatic, having interests in football, cycling and boxing and all the country pursuits. Of these, my inclination was cycling and very soon I went to Loughborough and bought a bike. The price shook me, four pounds, nineteen shillings and eleven pence (£4.19.11d) of which I had two pounds ten shillings. I gave the man the money and said I would bring the rest of the price on the first of the month which was next pay day. He said, "I suppose it would be useful to have the machine at your job? You are a bit out of town." I said it would as the bus service was sparse, so he told me to take the machine with me and keep to our agreement on pay day.

I dithered a bit as dad's shadow came between me and the bike

("Have nothing you can't pay for") but finally decided he was far enough away for me to get on with things myself and proudly rode back to Beau Manor in high delight.

Well, we all know that pride goes before the fall, and as I entered the gravel drive I felt the back wheel skid under me and I fell.

My arrival back in the kitchen put the cook in a tizzy and further expeditions were banned, two bloody knees and a grazed elbow being cited as a good reason. I managed to put up a good argument about the gravel being very thick where it met the tarmac, and although she did not rescind the order I could see she was wavering a bit so I judged it wise to say no more. Shortly after my half day came round and Bunny and I decided to have a ride to Derby to see dad's sister, Nell.

The lunch was late, and I was working until two thirty rushing to get finished and out as we had a long ride ahead of us. The day was a rare one and we whistled and sang all the latest songs as we went, I think then it was *Blue moon, When the poppies bloom again* and *The Continental.*

We had time for a leisurly tea and a short game with the young cousins and it was time to turn our steeds for the return trip. It was necessary to leave in plenty of time as I had to be in at ten sharp.

It was the footman's job to answer the door for those who were out. It was not possible to enter the house by stealth, if someone was late he knew about it and he made a special effort to see that the fact was well advertised.

Having enjoyed my outing to Derby, I thought a nice ride out next Sunday morning, while the others were at church, would suit me well and when they set off to church I wheeled the machine out of the shed and passed them on the drive. Some of them would have liked to go with me but were afraid of a dressing down if they were not seen to be in church, so I rode on to look at the Beacon, walked up to enjoy the view and then it was time to go back to see to the lunch. I was ready with the others, preparations followed the usual lines, and no-one mentioned my absence; coffee went in and things took a slower pace as we began to clear up the disarry, when down came the Awful Alfred full of cheer that someone was due for a rocket.

With devilish glee he said loudly, "The old girl wants to see our Joanie on the drawing room carpet."

"Now?" I said.

"Sooner than that," he said, hoping to terrify me to tears. I walked to my drawer in the old dresser, took out a clean apron which we always kept for a forray through the front and sallied forth to see the Hon. Mrs.

Approaching the drawing-room, I found Alfred hanging about in the corridor wearing an expectant expression. I thought, "I'll fix you mate," and when I was told to "Come in" I made certain the door was firmly shut behind me.

The Hon. Mrs. was reclining on the chesterfield, a peke on her lap and smoking a cigarette in a long holder. Eyeing me as I crossed the carpet, the silence began to make me nervous and I said, "You wished to see me Madam?"

Removing the holder from her lips, she leaned forward to place it on an ashtray on the small table. "Indeed I do wish to see you. I wish you to explain your absence from church this morning."

"There is nothing to explain," I said, "I decided to go for a cycle ride instead."

The Hon. Mrs. looked at me in amazement as though she could hardly believe her ears. "Was there a special reason for your absence?" she said quietly, with her natural feelings well disciplined.

"Only that it was such a lovely morning that I thought it was silly to sit inside when I could go out for a ride."

"But," said the good lady, "You know perfectly well that you are given the Sunday morning specifically to attend church."

I had been recalling mum's words before leaving home, "Don't be agressive or pushy. You can make your point without being cheeky, but if you feel right is on your side don't be afraid to say so." I mentally checked the list and decided I had met her criteria and came back to the matter in hand in time to hear the tail of a sentence, "and I don't want this to happen again. Do you understand?"

"I will go to church if it is a special service like Easter or Christmas," I said, "but mostly I shall go for a ride," making my position clear.

The Hon. Mrs. so far forgot herself as to raise her voice, "Are you stupid or are you just not listening? I repeat this will not happen again. If it does, your bicycle will be confiscated. DO YOU UNDERSTAND?"

"But it is my property," I said reasonably, "I worked hard and saved the money. Anyone can have a bike."

"How old are you?"

"Seventeen," I said.

"I cannot think you are unintelligent," she went on, "but I shall tell you again. You will attend church. You may go back to your duties."

I stood there for a second, thinking there must be something else I could say to make her see reason. I felt the whole episode to be quite unfair, and besides, my bike was the pride of my life.

"You wished to say something?" she asked as I stood there.

"Yes," I said, "If we MUST go to church then its not time off. I shall stay in my room."

I recall that I was suprised to see the good lady flumoxed. Prehaps she glimpsed the demise of her way of life in that incident. I closed the door and went back to the kitchen, and the girls crowded round to see if Alfred had indeed been right and I had been given a moment's notice.

The cook wanted to know all about it, and I had the impression that she was not as cross as I had expected her to be. Her final comment was that she had no wish to lose me but it might be impossible to override the Hon. Mrs's wishes in the matter. We young ones were nonplussed that our cook had not been on the side of the Mrs.

I discovered later that my bacon had been saved by the cook's glowing account of my work and general behaviour, and later on I thought how times had changed. In earlier days instant dismissal and no references would have been the order of the day.

My next two Sunday mornings off were spent as I said they would be in my room, but by the next time it had been announced that attendence at church would be welcomed; those who wished to do other things on their Sunday mornings were at liberty to do so.

Soon after this my mother was ill and I left to go home to look after dad and the dogs, regretfully, as I had enjoyed my time there, and also I was sorry to leave Bunny's family who had taken me in as one of their own.

There were several litters of Scotties about and there was a lot to do in the kennels, but the biggest part was the exercising of the dogs up to the Heath, to Primrose Hill, or to Parliment Hill Fields. We were well known in the area, my mother as the "Dog Lady" and I as "Dog Lady's daughter." I was thankful that my dad was not a rat-catcher.

Dolly, who had been my friend for several years, was glad to see me back home and we decided to buy a second-hand car. It was becoming fashionable for 'ordinary' people to own cars; up to then if you had a well off relative who arrived by car the local kids from blocks around would congregate to stroke the bonnet or polish the radiator cap with a sleeve and when the driver appeared there was a chorus "Give us a ride guv'nor," and sometimes their luck was in.

We asked around and found we could buy an old Austin Seven for five pounds, so we worked out ways and means, but forgot running costs and petrol, so we shelved the idea.

Our next inspiration was a day trip to Dunkirk. The thought of 'going abroad' was intoxicating; at that time the only folk to travel were the rich, the army and those who emigrated. We were, in a way, trail-blazers, as much pioneers as those of the old West. We would be the first in either family to 'go foreign' except those who had fought for king and country.

On the day we sallied forth to Victoria Station to get the boat train. We were damned from the start. A long wait for the bus, a long queue at the ticket office, only to be told "Next window please," then somebody asked if we had changed our money. What did they mean "change our money?"

"Into French francs." they said.

"Not likely," we said, "if the French don't like our money we shan't go." So we went to Oxford Street instead. We bought something for supper and set about the serious business of buying a dress each, out of our day trip money.

We were at Lyons Corner House when we noticed that Gracie Fields was in *Sing as we go* at the Regal, Marble Arch and we decided we would have a shot at that. We had a seat in the balcony as we were flush for money; they cost one and nine, and as we usually paid ninepence this was a taste of the high life.

As the film had not yet started the place was almost empty and there was one man sitting slightly to our right four rows down. We had our sweets and were enjoying our film when Dolly dug me in the ribs with her elbow.

"What's the matter?" I hissed. She gestured with her thumb and I saw that the man had moved up till he was seated immediately in front of her. We gathered our stuff together and moved along to the end of the row, where she took off her shoes again and made herself comfortable.

Within fifteen minutes she dug me in the ribs again. I looked at her in the murk and she nodded forward; this chap had moved again to the seat in front of Dolly and was now holding her foot in his hand. She waited for me to see it and then snatched her foot away. I had a job to control my laughter when there was a thud and a stifled yell, and I glanced sideways to see Dolly had her shoe in her hand, the man was rubbing his wrist and was rapidly making for the exit.

We saw the rest of the film with no further incident and came out to have a pot of tea and a chocolate cream bun in Joe Lyons and made our slow way home window gazing as we went. We had bought a dress, had lunch and tea, bought our supper, and had a three and a half hour picture show and were left with a small amount of change for our car kitty, which we still thought a good idea, but one which never came to fruition; Dolly's husband had his first car in 1949 and George had his in 1970, but drove it only eighteen months before his ill health forced him to give it up.

By this time the war clouds were gathering and there was much talk of gas masks and air-raid precautions and a friend, May, had gone off to train in the navy. Mum had recovered from her bout of ill health and I went into a temporary place in Park Street while the cook was in hospital and following that I was a temp in Wilton Place while the kitchen-maid went home to nurse her mother and then I had to decide where I went from there. In view of the fact that war appeared imminent, I thought I would get a day job to be near home, so I answered an ad in our local paper.

The house was a modest three-bedroom affair and a bit of a come-down after the houses I had been in, but it was a good move and I was very happy there and learned a great deal. The family were German Jewish refugees and had arrived in England in 1935 with only what they could put in the small car, which had given up five miles out of Dover. When I met them they were just beginning to pull themselves up by their boot laces and my interest in things foreign was stimulated by their story which was the classic one of persecution in business, at home, by neighbours and in the school, and although they had lost almost all they owned, when I arrived on the scene, they had got as far as the little house, and a miniscule workroom in Margaret Street. *Haute couture* was all Mr F. knew and he was cutting, machining and buying and his wife did the finishing, modelling, cleaning and the accounts. The designing and the delivering they did together.

We had taken to each other at once and I was fascinated to hear their tales of Germany and the rest of Europe, which the family had visited in happier times. In due course I met a number of relatives and their families who passed through *en route* to Canada, U.S.A., Ireland, Mexico and South America.

One family came from Moscow, the father being a doctor, the mother was a chiropodist, and they had flown to Moscow, thinking a safe haven was there, but when details of the pact between the Russian bear and the German eagle emerged, the family knew it was time to move on.

War came closer and I joined the A.R.P. As events took shape Dolly and I realised that our travels would have to be shelved for the duration. "After the war." we said and sometimes, "Maybe it won't come to anything", but the last holiday I had was a week before the declaration of hostilities. I thought that would be the end of my travels until peace was restored but I was wrong.

The German couple went off to the internment camp on the Isle of Man. I did three months on nights with my partner in the A.R.P. Dad fire-watched every night for months on end, making sure his horses were as safe as possible; mum's sister did her stint at the telephone exchange in Kensington; my youngest uncle joined the Auxuliary Fire Service in Finchley; and the remaining uncle fire-watched at Paddington Station, so we didn't meet for months at a time.

George and I had been going out together for quite some time and we decided to marry. As he was working in Luton and I was in London, with our lives so changed we met seldom and plans were made at long distance. But one day he could come to London on his motor bike. I had a meal ready, in my bedsit, but he failed to arrive, and when the phone finally rang it was to say he had lost three fingers on his left hand. He had been preparing the machine for the road when his hand slipped off the back step and into the driving chain.

When he recovered from this, George was back on the job ploughing up everything that could be ploughed, often working by moonlight as tractors then had no lights or cabins, and after years in the doldrums farmers were having things easier moneywise. The government began to pay two pounds an acre for pasture to be turned to arable land in order to produce food for the nation. Even the public parks were turned into allotments and 'townies' began

41

to grow their own vegetables.

"Dig for victory" posters were everywhere, as were "Be like dad-keep mum", "Careless talk costs lives" and "Coughs and sneezes spread diseases."

We thought things would be difficult from a financial viewpoint, but a cottage went with his job and the farmer had promised a reasonable wage.

I knew my dad could be very awkward, so I cut my cloth accordingly, telling George we must do it all by the book. I asked dad if George could come to the house to talk to him about us getting married. To the surprise of both mum and myself he said agreeably, "Yes, tell him to come for dinner on Sunday."

Came the great day, mum and I were nervous as cats, and from past experience we felt there was a catch in it, although we were thankful all appeared calm. George arrived at the appointed time and we had our lunch with a bit of general conversation, and after the meal, by pre-arrangement mum and I cleared the table and left the men to talk. Forty minutes later, we produced a tray of tea and apprehensively took it in. I looked at George and asked the unspoken question. Under cover of lighting a cigarette he did a 'thumbs up'. The dark cloud lifted and I began to feel more comfortable. An hour later we took our leave and walked to Hampstead Heath, where we discussed the amazing day.

It was hard for someone outside the family to first believe and then to understand such worry and misery that my mother and I endured as a regular thing. Inevitably like many people before him, George said, "Why do you get so scared of your old man? He was O.K. very pleasant." I was just happy that all had gone well, unaware of the bombshell about to drop.

Next day I left work early to go to St. Pancras Town Hall to put the notice in for the wedding. Particulars were taken and a form produced which I had to give to my father to sign saying he gave permission for his daughter to marry. In 1940 I was twenty and a half and the age at which one could marry without parental consent was twenty-one.

When dad came in for his dinner I produced the form and a pen and asked him to sign where the cross was. He said, "What's all this for then?"

I earnestly explained that the registrar had sent it because he was unable to marry us without dad's signature to say that he agreed to the marriage.

"Yes," he agreed, "that's right, he can't can he?"

Again I proffered the pen and said, "He's put a cross where you have to sign." Suddenly I knew I was flogging a dead horse, and in that instant dad said, "I don't have to sign anything."

I looked at the smile on on the face of the crocodile and knew he had planned it like this right from the moment I had asked if George could come to see him.

In the certain knowledge that the matter was closed as far as he was concerned having shown me that he was the guv'nor, yet still I endeavoured to straighten the matter out, I said, "If you don't sign the form then we can't marry until after my birthday."

"That's right," he said with a sarcastic smile. I looked at my mother's stricken face; we both knew that although I had her sympathy, no help would be forthcoming. She was always scared of him, although he had never abused her in a physical way. Mental cruelty had been his weapon, there and then I decided enough was enough and, come what may, this was one battle I was going to win. Mum and I had been humiliated and embarrassed before family and friends for years and this was to be the last time. Now he was due for a taste of his own medicine.

Saying nothing to anyone I took myself off to Marylebone Magistrates Court and asked to see the Court Missionary. He or she would be one of a vast army of wealthy or upper middle class folk who gave unstintingly of their free time to help the less well off with their problems. In this case the middle aged daughter of a general attended the court daily to assist with legal matters.

I was ushered into this lady's office and was asked to sit. I told my story in full and she said that she would need to come to the house and speak to my father to discover the reasons for his objections. I replied that he had no objections or how could he agree with George the previous day? I also said I wished to apply for a magistrate's permission in lieu of my father's and that a home visit would be fraught with difficulties, owing to his uncertain temper. He could well be rude to her; she smiled and said that she had batted on sticky wickets before and lived to tell the tale. My private thought was that she had never seen a sticky wicket, but it was arranged that she would call the next evening at six-thirty. I told Mum what I had done and her apprehension was obvious as we discussed the matter.

"How can I tell him all this?" She said, "He'll go absolutely potty."

I said, bravely, "I'll tell him. You keep out of it."

I had no idea how this was to be accomplished knowing only too well the dry mouth, the shortage of breath , the thumping heart and the damp forehead which had accompanied previous confrontations.

I thought I could tell him during the lunch hour next day and felt better after having made the decision, then went round to Dolly's house to tell her what I had done. She was aghast and told her mum, who was a very straightforward lady and having heard the woeful tale said, "What does the silly old B think he's going to gain from these antics?".

By the hour of doom the next day I had still not had the courage to say my piece. Dad had been his usual awkward self and before the deed was done the doorbell rang. As I went to answer the door I heard him say to no one in particular, "Who the hell's that just when I want to read the paper?' I let the lady in saying, "My Dad's in a bad temper and I'm afraid he'll be very nasty when he knows what you have come for."

"Don't worry," she smiled, "all will be well, you'll see." Dad met us on the top of the steps saying "Who are?" but she forestalled him saying, "Good evening. I'm from the Magistrate's court." He ignored the outstretched hand and went into the sitting room and we followed. I wished the floor would open and swallow me. I felt sick and every nerve was jangling in the well known way.

"So what are you doing here then?" he asked.

"I have come to talk about your daughter's marriage," she said. He turned a baleful glance in my direction before asking, "What the devil is that to do with you?"

"I understand you first gave consent in conversation and later refused to sign the consent form?"

"What bloody business is it of yours?" he roared thrusting his face close to hers. "You may get out of my house 'toot sweet'", using a favourite expression.

"Mr Renwick, may I appeal to you-."

"No you may not." he bellowed, "and get your arse out of here and get back from where you came. When I want you I'll send for you. Get out before I throw you out."

By now he was leaning over her in a very menacing fashion. She gathered her gloves, handbag and clip board and rose from her seat;

I was almost fainting with tension but with her face level with his, she said in a very quiet voice, "In view of the fact that I am from the Magistrate's court you would be ill advised to contemplate doing anything silly." and putting her arm across my shoulder and looking at Dad directly as she faced him, she continued, "I would like to see you in my office tomorrow Miss Renwick, perhaps about two-thirty if you can manage that, and I shall hope to see you looking much better than you do at the moment dear". I led the way to the front door apologising for the awful interview upstairs.

"That's alright my dear. I have been in much more difficult situations than that." and this time I believed her.

The meeting next day was short; she took all details of Georges job and possible prospects and advised me that it would be helpful if he could write a letter to the court outlining his work, overtime and the accommodation we would have and anything else we felt might be relevant to the matter and bring it to the court hearing at the time appointed.

She would set the wheels in motion and in a day or two a summons would be delivered to my father to appear in court to defend his decision to withold his consent.

She felt it would be better if, as far as possible, I stayed out of dad's way, so as to not get involved in arguments and in the event of close contact, not to attempt to justify my actions in going to the court. That was the last time I saw her and the summons came two days later, delivered by a bobby in uniform. My mother nearly died on the spot, because if you got a summons it was almost as bad as going into Pentonville. She shook so much she could hardly hold the pen, so I signed as having received the long envelope and placed it on the sideboard where all dad's mail was put.

Dad read it as soon as he arrived home for his lunch and never addressed another word to me from then, mid January, until my birthday in August.

When the day came to appear at court Dolly came to give moral support; it was snowing thickly and very cold and all the trouble had made me very nervous and I could keep nothing down. Neither of us had been in court before. In 1939 decent working class folk had no truck with courts, as a consequence we were filled with terror.

We were amazed to find the place we were in was packed with people and the noise was unbelievable. Amid the hubbub stentorian voices were calling names and suddenly one I recognised. "Joseph

Charles Renwick." I looked quickly around but there was no sign of my dad. After another fifteen minutes scanning the crowd I heard another name. "Eunice Joan Renwick." Dolly said, "I'll wait here for you." and I followed the usher into the courtroom.

My heart sank as I immediately recognised the man in the great carved chair on the bench. He was famous as all readers of the *Evening News* knew well. The paper ran a daily column called 'The courts day by day' and his satirical wit and sarcasm poured over the heads of drunks, vagrants, prostitutes and their pimps, made highly entertaining reading, but faced with this man I could only wish that the ground would open and I could disappear into the chasm.

This terrifying personage leaned over the edge of the bench, listening to the clerk of the court, who had a sheaf of papers in his hand; as the clerk moved away the magistrate looked fully towards me and I felt myself shrivel on the instant.

"Where is your father?" were his opening words.

"I don't know," was all I could manage.

"Speak up," he bellowed. "Where is your father?"

"I don't know," I said again.

"Is that all you are capable of saying? Is your father coming into court to give his objections to this business?"

By now I was stung into pulling myself together and answered, "I have to say I don't know. My father has not spoken to me since the summons came."

"What age are you?" he snapped.

"Twenty-one in August," I told him.

"Take this young lady away and give her her permission. The court's time is not to be wasted," he rasped.

In a flash I was out of the court and into the office where a man was already filling in a parchment to which he affixed a big red seal. He rolled it up, placed it in a cylinder and handed it to me with a smile. "There you are my dear," he said, "Best of luck to you both."

We came out of the building wondering why there had been so much palaver and nastiness over the matter, but, ours is not to reason why, and we parted company. Dolly to go to work and I to take the precious document to the registrar at the Town Hall.

He congratulated me on the success of the affair and we set a date for the wedding. He gave me another form for my mother's signature, which suprised me somewhat, thinking the magistrate's intervention would stand in lieu of both parents agreement. Having had all this explained to me I left the Town Hall and returned home to get somthing to eat. Then I began to remember father and how he would be when I got back and the old familiar nervous shivering beset me once more.

I need not have worried on that score; he had lunched early and gone again so I had ample time to tell mum all that had taken place. Eventually I said, "So I've arranged the date for a month's time and I've just got to take the other form back to the registrar and we're all set up."

"That's good," she said, "What's the other form for?"

Not sensing the new pit yawning at my feet I said, "It's the same as the one dad wouldn't sign. The registrar put a cross where you have to sign."

"ME?" she said, her voice high with panic. "I can't do it. He'll kill me. I'm sorry, Joanie, I can't sign it."

"Then how do I get married?" I asked her.

She shook her head. "I can't do it, really I can't." A short pause ensued, then she said, "Prehaps it would be better to wait."

The pause had been long enough for my brain to think up and then reject several courses of action, and the years of defeat, humiliation, ridicule and misery, fused together and became such an imprenetrable barrier that I knew I had seen the last of dad's ridiculous regime. I picked up the pen and said to my mum, "If you don't sign for me, I shall just go to Luton and live with George." Her face wet with tears, she took the pen and signed her name.

As if all that were not enough to endure, word came that George was in hospital with pneumonia, and as a result our wedding took place later, on 6th April 1940. On the morning of the great day my dad was still in the house at nine fifteen, two hours after his normal time of leaving for work and mum was at her wits end waiting for him to leave so she could get ready to go to the registry office.

None of dad's folks came down for the wedding, there was nothing to come for with him being like he was; there was no reception and no party, but I had reckoned without all my old collegues at the A.R.P. posts around the area. All those who were off duty were on parade and the four year old son of one was all kitted out as a miniature warden in boiler suit, with tin hat, gas mask, whistle, rattle and canvas bag, and the whole company adjourned to the A.R.P. canteen in Camden Town. Bangers and mash and a great time was had by all.

47

Of course, everyone knew about dad and his peculiarities and I was grateful that so many people had done so much to make our day such a happy one.

Still, we were not to have a smooth passage in our new life. The promised wage never materialised and after four months of promises and excuses we decided to look elsewhere for a job.

Before we got fixed up Hitler's Luftwaffe flattened Grandma Quant's garden flat in Hamstead; luckily she was with her daughter in Yeovil and Aunty Ad arrived back from night work in the telephone exchange to find nothing left of her home but a wardrobe and her dressing-table, which had been miraculously preserved by a roof timber falling across it; this illustrated to me personally the old saying "It's an ill wind", as both these items came down to us before we moved to our next place.

Chapter Five

The new employment was on a dairy farm about three miles from Nuneaton; it could have been High Street, China, for the time it took to make arrangements. Post was delayed, phone lines were down and by the time we moved Coventry had been devastated. This time my journey was in a cattle truck the day after the big raid and long before we approached the city we were sickened by the awful smell, and although we made a detour we saw digging parties still on rescue duty, piles of rubble burning and columns of smoke rising from the ruins.

We were there two and a half years, during which time our elder daughter, Elizabeth, was born. We were again in a tied cottage, no light, no water in the house and the toilet at the far end of the garden beyond the pump.

We were fairly close to Derby and dad's sister, Nell, and her family came for a weekend; as soon as they arrived my uncle said, "I'll put the tickets under the pot rabbit on the mantel. Don't let me go off without them, Joan."

Well, guess what? Of course we went off without them; we had got four children and our baby ready for a two mile walk to the bus stop, and while waiting for the bus, we remembered the said tickets. There was consternation all round when George said, "I'll go back for them. I'll see you at the station," and off he went at a dog trot across the fields. We watched him till the bus arrived and we all got in, nobody saying much and thinking it was a forlorn exercise.

The kids kept looking behind the bus and reported no sign of pursuit and once on the station we explained all to the man at the barrier, who said he would look out for George and let him through at once.

The train came in, "Goodbyes" and "thanks" were called and Uncle Alec ushered the last one in as George thundered across the wooden bridge and down the steps, thrusting the tickets into the outstretched hand as the train moved away from the platform. Well, we all know that heroes have to be rewarded for the deeds of

49

derring-do they perform and that day my aunt awarded George the 'Order of the Fruit Cake' and from that day whenever there was movement of personnel in either direction between Derby and us a large fruit cake was the first item to be unpacked on arrival in our house. Sons, daughters, nephews and neices, were all press-ganged into service to deliver 'George's Cake'. On my first visit after George died there was the cake.

I said, "You've been paying this debt for thirty years now. It's time to stop." But seven years after he left us, George's cake still comes up. Nell has ten grandchildren and four great-grandchildren, all of whom know of the legendary George and how he brought the rail tickets from Marston Jabbet to Nuneaton, and the steed which carried him in such record time was the one that caused so much trouble at Beau Manor; it finally gave in aged twenty-nine years.

We had always been short of money, and farm wages being notoriously bad we tried for another job with better wages.

George spoke to the bailiff on the phone, and it all sounded so good he took the job without an interview and consequently without seeing the house.

Having moved, again in the cattle truck, the first item on the agenda was tea. Oh how marvellous to have water in the house at the sink; I rummaged about for the kettle, thinking how well things had turned out, until I got to the sink. We did indeed have water at the sink, but nobody warned us the water came out at such a terrifying speed. To be exact, a bucket had to stand under the tap all day in order to have enough water to bale out into the kettle or saucepan. We were not there long enough to discover what detriment the water system suffered from.

At this time we had two dogs, Sylvi, an Alsatian and Twerp, a Scottie, and these two had a daily ritual.

To the left of the front gate, there was a balloon site manned by a squad of W.A.A.F.s and to the right an anti-aircraft gun manned by the army. I always let the dogs out as soon as I got up and they would march abreast to the gate where they parted, the one on the left going to the left and the one on the right going to the right, where they each had breakfast with that particular squad, following which, ten minutes after, they could be seen passing each other at the front gate, each going to the opposite camp for breakfast. This habit never varied while we lived there and the dogs never visited either camp at any other time.

They were better fed than we were at this time, in fact mum used to send us a pound of sausages from time to time, and sometimes they were so long in the post that, by their arrival, its a wonder they were not self propelled.

Another shock came on our second day there. George came in from work and I asked what sort of day he had had, and he replied that he had thought yesterday that the job was not for him and today he was sure of it. It seemed all the staff were backbiting and at each other's throats and that was never George's style, so in six months we were off again.

This time we went for an interview and saw the house, which we liked. In years gone by it had been a pub for the bargees on the canal; in fact, the cottage was built over the famous canal tunnel which the boat people had to negotiate by lying on their backs on the cabin roof and pushing along with their feet on the roof of the tunnel.

We stayed there two years, just long enough to kill all the fleas which were breeding in the floor boards in the spare room. Every two days I boiled water in the copper and poured it over the floor and in between I doused it in Jeyes fluid. We also had rats which danced a fandango in hobnailed boots in the middle of the night, but even so, we loved it (after the lodgers had been dealt with.). Still, we had a pump and an outside toilet, but we did have electric light, so I felt we were making some progress. We kept pigs and chickens, and Janet was born there six months before we moved.

This time we had water and electricity in the house, but only for lighting, so I was still cooking on an oil stove. Once again we had the most lovely views and a rabbit field where we could go at any time of the day, stand at the gate, clap our hands and see dozens of white bunny scuts bobbing away to their burrows. Apart from the farmer, who was separated from us by the sheds and yards, we had no neighbours. The children had a long walk to school and they had bikes at the earliest opportunity.

Until then we all went on George's old bike which dad had given him when he bought himself a moped. We had no bus service from the village, except one morning and one afternoon bus on market day, which was Thursdays, so Shank's pony was the chief mode of transport.

Private cars had to be laid up for lack of petrol or given to the war effort, together with all iron railings, saucepans, kettles, bedsteads and any other metal items.

During this period George's nephew, Dick, came to stay for the first time. We think he enjoyed it as they came three times a year for all the years since, and are still making the journey. Dick spent all his war service in the notorious 'Fly Bomb Alley' and came home every weekend, but Nemesis finally caught up with him when his mob sailed for India on the very day all hostilities ceased. On his return after a year away, I discovered that I had only suppressed my interest in foreign travel, and listening to all that he had seen and done in India only kindled the flame anew, although I had reached the stage where I believed the itch in my feet would never be alleviated.

The children needed more and more, wages never expanded at the rate required, even though I worked in local houses and on the farm at busy times, so ever a realist, I settled down to be an armchair traveller and in the next fifteen years I read of all these fascinating places, while the foreign holiday bubble exploded around me.

Our holidays were never arranged like other folk arranged theirs. Winter holidays were for us, "You take Xmas week, George" and no arguing, so with this pattern established, I went to London in the summer to look after the dogs, while mum and dad went to Lymington to my aunt; dad paid our fares, so we were not out of pocket, but for our week at Christmas our chickens paid the bill and for our gifts too.

We had kept layers for some years in order to have fresh eggs during the shortages and any not needed at the time would be pickled in a bucket of preservative to be used for cooking cakes at a later date; we then thought we would run some cockerels fattening them for Chistmas.

This meant we would need to stay up three nights, well into the small hours to get the birds all plucked and dressed ready to take them down to the family and friends in time for the festivities. People were so glad to have country fresh food during time of shortage that we could have sold hundreds if we had them. Folk would be at my mother's door asking if there were any spares. Each one had a home to go to from when they were chicks.

The first task was to deliver the birds, when we also collected the money, which took all the first evening and the next morning, because the chickens went to destinations in several parts in London; after that we were free to visit all the uncles and aunts,

Dolly and her folks and May's mum and dad who always had May's latest letters for me to read. They knew of my itch to travel and that I drank in all the descriptions of May's doing in Colombo and Singapore, from where she was lucky to escape, some older family friends were taken prisoner by the Japanese.

Christmas Day was spent at home with mum and dad, but Boxing Day meant an early start, because all the family congregated at 'Tally Ho Corner', where mum's youngest brother lived. This house obviously had elastic gussets, or how could we have got in otherwise?

There were grans, grandpas, uncles, aunts, cousins, nephews, brothers and sisters, In-laws, and In-laws of In-laws, and maybe an odd out-law to whom we never drew attention.

Apart from demolishing the fruits of Aunty Con's labours at meal times, we entertained ourselves with games, singsongs, forfeits, solos by voice, violin, piano, or piano-accordion, and once we had a ten piece band which included a biscuit tin and a comb and paper.

Some of those who lived away in the country would have their fares paid by those who had better jobs in London, in order that the whole family could enjoy the festival together, and this was not an isolated, one off thing, but went on for years and years.

There were no dishwashers, few washing machines, not many people had a carpet cleaner, unless it was a Ewbank sweeper, and we young marrieds of the time can see now, how times were happier and more relaxed and the hang-ups of today were not in everyday conversations.

Some folk say our present troubles stem from nuclear weapons hanging over us, but we lived with the threat of gas warfare, and rockets and doodlebugs which were no more conventional then, than nuclear filth is now.

We had another change of job, still in the Banbury area and this time, right in the village, and for the first time I had a next door neighbour, which worried me a bit, never having had one before, but we became good friends at once and have remained so for thirty-three years.

We had loads of visitors; all the young cousins from Derby came with girl and boyfriends, who suddenly became husbands and wives, the cousins from Somerset stayed the night for Silverstone, suddenly we were thinking of Be leaving school. She needed to do typing, but before we got as far as a typewriter for her, George had a terrible accident on the farm. He and the man he worked with, a Yugoslav ex-prisoner of war, had brought up a bull calf, which was such a pet that he ran behind them like a dog as they moved about the farm. The time came to move this young Bovril out to a pasture with other young stock and they were sorry to lose him. They missed having him around, but eventually the time came to bring him back to the yard, so George and Lou, armed with the regulation pole, went to get him.

Lou had other work to do so George brought the animal back alone and decided not to use the pole, just the halter on the bull's head. Halfway to the farm, the bull pushed his head into George's back, knocking him down. Picking himself up, he said to the creature, "What the hell did you do that for?" caught the halter rope, took a pace forward and the animal did it again. Everyone thinks of being gored by a bull, but in this case, having knocked George down he lowered his great head onto George's chest and pushed, breaking a great many ribs one of which punctured a lung and damaged his liver.

The friend, having finished feeding young stock, came over the hill and saw the bull in the middle of the field apparently alone. Mystified, he watched for a moment till the bull took a couple of paces back and then Lou saw what seemed to be a bundle on the ground. As the bull moved forward to attack, truth dawned and he raced forward to the scene. By the time he arrived George had dreadful injuries and was quite unconscious. Each time he moaned the bull moved in again, so giving him a whack across the nose, Lou picked the inert mass up and struggled across a small stream, laid George under a bush and ran to the farm for help.

At first all appeared lost, but three weeks at the Horton General and several weeks at home, and he was back at work, never the same again, but able to do most of the jobs expected of him. Some months after he started back he discovered he had a torn shoulder muscle, and this prevented him doing all the work he should have done, but when he got to something he was unable to manage one of the other men took it over. Meanwhile, the bull had gone off to the Bovril factory and the police had recommended Lou for the Queen's medal for Brave Conduct which he received at Oxford from the Minister for Agriculture and Fisheries.

Naturally all this set us back from a money standpoint, and things we had hoped to do got shelved; I did extra work on the farm until we picked ourselves off the floor. Then Be decided she would like to train at Debenham and Freebody as a dressmaker, which entailed apprenticeship in Wigmore Street.

I felt we would never get out of the rut we were in; I was always making and mending, and we still helped Elizabeth in London, as she was only earning enough to pay her keep at Dolly's, where she was living.

To make things worse for me on a personal level the folk I worked for in the next village were off on a business cum holiday trip to Australia, returning by way of South Africa and the names of the places they were to visit made my scalp tingle and I yearned to be able to see some of the world. The Blue Mountains, the Nullabor Plain, Sydney and Alice Springs had me looking in the atlas and I vowed not for the first time, that I would take off sometime even if I died in the attempt.

By Christmas '59 Be had finished her training and came back to find a job, only to be disappointed, as there was no work of the calibre she had been trained for. All she could get was lifting and lowering of hems, or letting out waists, or altering zips. Having explored all possibilities, she went to the wig makers, a job she enjoyed doing. She had a steady boyfriend and wedding plans were being made for two or three years hence.

In January '60 our world went mad. We had three deaths in the family in eleven days, the first of which was my mother, which posed the question, "What will dad do?" He had recently bought a cottage property at Bodicote for his retirement, but my mother had said she knew she would never live there; in fact the builders began work on it on 4th January and mum died on the twentieth.

Having dealt with the last of the funerals the tide of our affairs changed rapidly, and we found ourselves buying our own house. I had never imagined living in anything other than a farm worker's cottage 'till the day I died, but George had found increasing difficulty with the work and relied even more on his friend to help him out. He thought he might do better in the factory in Banbury, the snag being that leaving farm employment meant leaving the house that went with the job.

As luck had it, Lou, who was a dedicated budgie breeder by now, had a slight altercation with the boss, who made some snide remark about the birds which enraged Lou so much that he came in breathing fire and declaring enough was enough.

From these small beginnings grew the idea of pooling our resources, if the right property could be found. It came to light without us looking for it, and from then on we were carried along on a tide over which we had no control. Problems came up and were smoothed away; we were sent to a person who was sorry he could not help us with a mortgage, but pop and see Mr. So and So, he may think of something helpful, and he did. We had crisis after crisis and were alternately cast down and lifted up, cheered and depressed, and always the path was made smooth. We had been rejected by two building societies, refused a loan by my dad and a friend of twenty-five years, when finally I was sent to a bank manager by an estate agent as a last resort, and the bank manager fell over himself to lend us the money. I had no idea if I was on foot or horseback as we scraped the bottoms of all our barrels to find the deposit. Lou sold several of his best birds, the money George had been given as a lump sum, instead of a weekly pension at the time of the accident was withdrawn from the bank, I realised three premium bonds and between us we had the magnificent sum of two hundred and fifty pounds.

Then it was time to organise the move, and to keep costs down, our coal-man moved us in his lorry, which was hardly an auspicious start, although it was hilarious all the way, then even before the house was straight there was a *cri de coeur* from a friend who had lost her husband when my mum had died, asking me to go on holiday with her as she was unable to face going alone, and if I would, then she would arrange everything and inform me in due course.

Although it was no time to be going on holiday, we all realised she was in dire straits so I agreed and the letter arrived with the dates and "Don't forget your passport." Passport? I thought her lid had flipped; I had imagined a week at Bournemouth, what did we need passports for? Holland, that's what! Dutch bulb fields; after all those years of wishing and hoping, with no real effort on my part, I was on my way.

Chapter Six

This tour began for me before I left home and a slight nervousness at the thought of flying was dissipated by the usual euphoria which seizes me at the thought of going.

The tour party when assembled was interesting, the same mix you can see anywhere at any airport. The sweet young thing hanging on the arm of a man who could be 'daddy' but isn't, a few elderly folk who are well used to travelling and some recently retired who are determined to "do things and go places" while still able, and the two characters who are always there, the well off woman who hogs the courier and the man who travels alone and is always late back to the coach with a slight list to starboard, no matter what time the transport is due to leave.

I recall little of the flight except that several of the party were trying to prop up the bar before it was open; for myself, the sense of awe at being above the clouds has never left me, and if a plane flies over when I am in my garden, I am still amazed that people are walking about 'up above'.

I never realised until that Dutch trip how many lonely folk there are and package tours have their quota. Elsa, Dolly and I on other trips have heard harrowing stories of cruelty, injustice, ill health and devotion enough to fill a book, and we always seemed to attract these unattached folk.

However, the traveller we like least is the aggressive ungrateful one who will dismiss everything out of hand, as a waste of time, including an Aussie nurse, doing the old country and Europe by working her passage. She complained that putting all the flower heads on the floats was a complete waste of time; I wondered what she thought was the reason we had taken the trip in the first place, or if she realised that is how the Dutch advertise their expertise in the flower markets of the world.

That first foray into foreign travel remains rather hazy to me; I suppose because so much had happened in the five months since the beginning of the year, also the fact the holiday had come so

57

suddenly and in so unexpected a way that I was unable to digest it all.

I recall a stop for lunch on the outskirts of Alkmaar. As we came to rest outside the main door of this old timbered building, a gigantic figure appeared, attired in white from head to foot, with added height from a chef's hat, perched at an acute angle atop his shining pate. His enormous girth was encircled by a wide leather belt from which hung a large brass handled steel, and a large bunch of keys glinting as they caught the light. His ruddy face was split in a huge grin as he boomed, "Please to inkommen laydees an chentelmans. We are like to see you. I was in your country in the war. We like the English. We shall fill you with one good lunch." And did exactly that.

Goliath disappeared into the kitchen to supervise his minions and later passed among the tables, booming a word here and there, making sure everyone was receiving proper attention and had a good lunch. As we left to board our coach he ushered us out and stood waving us off 'till we were out of sight. Ripples of comment on the coach confirmed the satisfaction of all, and Elsa said, "He reminded me of the Laughing Cavalier,"

"No ," I said, "all I could think of was once round him, twice round the gasworks."

We visited the Floriade, which appeared to be the local park taken over by the local growers, who each have a large bed filled with his own speciality product. With blooms massed in such large areas, the impact of colour is considerable and breath-taking, and the nice thing was that we could order there and then.

As our plane came in at Schipol we had seen all these blocks of colour like children's building bricks and appreciated them again as we took the aerial car across the main road which divided the two parts of the park.

The clog maker held our interest as he picked his log from the pile at his feet and skilfully carved out the centre, sliced the point, and it seemed in no time at all there was the finished article, only needing a coat of paint before going on show for the tourist.

A visit to the Delft Pottery, came next and we both wanted to take things home for the family, but in the event the wall plates were quite dear, so we contented ourselves with small items and the memory of larger ones. We saw that the typical blue and white was black on entering the kiln, only getting its characteristic colour after baking.

The coach took us to a North Holland town called Volendam. A large number of the population, both men and women, wore national costume and we heard that the area is traditionally Catholic. The people were happy to explain their costumes to the strangers in their midst. Whether they were worn all year or only in the tourist season was not made clear. Most of the women and girls wore full black skirts and white blouses under an embroidered waistcoat, and high lace caps which had been in their families for generations, and were in fact, a considerable part of the family wealth. There was a great deal of silver and coral jewellery, also heirlooms, having connections with the Dutch colonies in the Far East. The costumes of the men consisted of full trousers, jackets in black and coloured shirts, blue, brown or red, with silver buttons and clogs completed the outfits.

At one stage our coach travelled for several miles parallel to the canal which was ten feet higher than the road, and it crossed my mind that if the worst happened and the bank did start to leak, we would be lucky to find a latter-day Peter to put his finger in the dyke.

Much has been written about the Dutch reclamation schemes, but to grasp the full meaning of the task they set themselves, one has to see the neat meadows for mile after mile, with fat Friesian cattle grazing the lush pastures. They showed us with pride the acres reclaimed from the sea and told of the next project.

Rotterdam was an experience which created wonder in us all as we were all of an age to remember the war first hand, we knew that the city had been razed to the ground by the Luftwaffe. A massive rebuilding programme had been going on since then, but we were unprepared for the marvellous new city centre which had risen from the ashes of the old.

We came across the sculpture in the grass commemorating the fate of the city. I and others were moved as we gazed at the sombre male figure with a great hole through his torso, which represents Rotterdam with the heart torn from it.

An intriguing trip to the top of the Euromast was the next item and several of the party crowded into the lift intending to sample the delights of the restaurant's gooey gateaux and coffee, with more cream than cake, and to see the view over the city.

Once in the lift there was much pushing and shoving as we all settled our carrier-bags and handbags, but before movement ceased the lift stopped and no-one moved to get out. "We're going to the top," said one. "So are we," said another. "Right, then. Everybody out," said our courier, laughing fit to burst. Some of them refused to believe we had reached the top and their expressions were comical, but eventually the lift emptied. We all wanted answers to queries about the height of the mast, the rate of ascent in the lift, cost of project, but it all became less and less interesting as the wonderful panorama of the port unfolded beneath us.

There were dozens of craft, looking like toy boats in a bath, moving about on the water, some in smart livery and others coming in after a long sea voyage looking like rusty old hulks, with many tugs huffing and puffing about getting their charges into position. Innumerable cranes were lifting all manner of cargo; cars, containers, timber, sacks and crates, all dipping, lifting, swinging and repeating the ritual time after time. Into my consciousness came Masefield's *Cargoes* and suddenly, *"smoke stacks"*, *"cheap tin trays"* and *"beating up the channel"* came alive.

Looking inland, there were other things to see, new roads, carrying hundreds of Dinky cars, toy houses with tiny lawns, surrounded with colour and many patches of green had a dark patch on them; the courier told us the children in school did a lot of sculpture and took their pieces home to be displayed by their families. Down at ground level we were able to see the sculptures at close hand and were amazed at the variety of talent and ideas displayed. Dull wood, shiny wood, stone, bronze and aluminium, but the greater number were of the wire coat-hanger and dustbin lid variety. Some of these could scarcely be classified as things of beauty, but one or two were quite fantastic. Most of us felt that the coat-hangers were put to better use in the flower floats built by the Dutch for their wonderful displays all over the country in the Spring.

We were privileged to see some remarkable creations, some as big as a house. There were swans, an elephant, cars, motor bikes, a castle, a crown on a cushion, a horse, all made from flower heads picked from the bulb at the appropriate moment in order to conserve the strength of the bulb to produce the beautiful flowers the next season.

A necessary part of a visit to Holland is a trip along Amsterdam's famous canals and gives the visitor a good view of the town houses, so tall and narrow that furniture has to be winched up by a pulley housed in the unique Dutch gable, and then taken in through the windows.

Years on, when Janet went to live in Schaesberg, I made many longer trips and have never got tired of the country or people. The former being so clean and the latter so friendly, I was sorry when Janet and her family moved.

On my second visit, which was with Dolly in 1966, we saw the Maduradam for the first time. We have the pioneer of model villages at Bourton on the Water, which has a special charm, then later Babbacombe constructed a model totally unlike the Cotswold project, which is a faithful copy of the real village, while Babbacombe, presumably, is an imaginary location, but one which I found completely captivating. The Maduradam is unlike either of these, being an urban representation with an airport, railway system, canal network and motorway plan, all models fully working. Planes taxi across the runway, trains run, barges glide and merchant shipping moves in the port. I am sure in the intervening years the model has been updated and improved. I always had this desire to take the "Big Five" to see these things but it was always a case of "next year maybe." But this particular dream was never realised and now we are at the stage where some of them can take their own young ones to see these miniatures.

Cornwall began to loom large in our life as Elsa was living there when she became ill with a terminal complaint; her sister and her family were living near me in the Midlands and we began to make more frequent journeys to help Elsa feel she was not totally isolated from her own people, so for a time our lives were geared up to deal with the new situation.

Pat and Tony would call for George and I after work on Friday, and we would travel down through the night. This meant that we always had time to fill before visiting the hospital, so we were able to see a great deal of the 'Old Kingdom', with its magical overlay of Druid stones, holy wells and legends, and until recently its old Celtic language related to Welsh and Breton which is entirely natural in the light of the fact that in the dim ages Wales, Cornwall and Brittany were one large land mass.

It seems that Cornish people have always been something of a mystery to the rest of the folk in these islands, perhaps because they were islanders within a nation of islanders, as Cornwall is surrounded by water as is any other island. For centuries, once the

61

Tamar was crosssed, the traveller felt the mystery of the land, and the romantic novelists have kept the pot boiling through the years. Advice to the early English was that "by Tre, Pol and Pen, ye shall know the Cornishmen," so perhaps in those days "forewarned was forearmed"

Whatever the truth of the matter, when Cornwall is mentioned, Tintagel is conjured up. There is an aura about the place which hits me each time I am there. The sea is always a Maelstrom and to see it is to know positively that nature is in charge and that man is of very little importance. Sinister dark rocks rear out of the boiling black sea which fills your ears with the sound of its fury as it has done for millions of years, and will no doubt, for millions more.

We visited tin mines, potteries, and Bodmin Moor, which we only saw through sheets of driving rain. We always said we would have a picnic on Bodmin, but only lunatics like ourselves would be at large on the moor in such weather.

By this time, Dolly and Vin had bought a bungalow on the Isle of Sheppy and both families had enjoyed the odd weekends and all the school holidays there. Something was always going on, an acre of lawn to be cut, or cement to be mixed, or a painting job, the borders to be worked on and everyone did a bit whilst enjoying the cliff top situation, with sea views and shipping activities. We all had a great deal of fun there, but Dolly and I were always ready to try something new, and when Vin announced he had been seconded to the army in Cyprus we were unable to believe our luck.

In the Spring of '62 the family took their leave of relations and friends, all vowing they would get out for the holidays as soon as the family were settled in their new home. The minute they went I went on an economy drive to get my fare and clothes together. The clothes were no problem as Elizabeth was a dress maker.

I did extra work and began putting money away for my air fare, but try as I might I found it an impossible task. Elizabeth had been married the previous year, but Janet was in the throes of various romances, and then decided to get herself engaged to "Fearless Fred," who was a great favourite with all of us.

The trouble was that Janet's fertile brain frequently went into spasm, bringing forth brilliant ideas which more often than not entailed the borrowing of money from mum, such as, "There is a nice bedroom suite for sale. I could squeeze it into my room until we are married." So I would withdraw the money, which never got put back and then I would have to clean her room while standing on one foot, because there was no room for both feet on the floor at the same time.

Concurrently, with the 'Janet and Fred' show George and I were struggling to get the house into a good state of repair. It had been very run down when we went in with the thatched roof leaking and all the windows and doors rotting and awaiting replacement. The garden had been like a jungle and was starting to look resonable and occupied, thus two years went by while I tried to regain lost ground, but even had I been able to get my economic requirements right, I would have been prevented from going to the "Island of Love", as civil unrest, fuelled by Grivas, had flared again. Eventually, when things had been quiet for several months, I had a letter, "It's now or never. We come home in May."

Gloomily I said to George, "I'll have to tell them I can't go!" As I was about to write the letter visitors arrived, so the unwelcome task was postponed. "I'll do it tomorrow," I said to myself, "when I come home from work."

Chapter Seven

Next day, in the butler's pantry, my employer came to discuss the day's work with me, when she suddenly asked when I had decided to go to Cyprus. I was staggered that she should mention it, as my own mind had been full of the subject.

"It's all off, I'm afraid," I said.

"Oh dear. I am sorry to hear that, you were so looking forward to it," she said.

I told her I had found it impossible for various reasons to get the fare together, although I was ready in all other respects.

"Are you half-way?" she asked. I told her the last thirty pounds had proved to be my Waterloo. "Poor old Joan," she said, and went off to see the kitchen staff.

Some hours later, as I was preparing to leave for home, my employer appeared again. Without preamble she said briskly, "I want you to make arrangements immediately to go to Cyprus," handing me a bit of paper. "Don't pay back cash. We will keep a record of your hours until it is worked off. The cheque is for thirty pounds plus five pounds pocket money. The five is a gift. Hurry, or your bus will be gone."

Equally brisk, I gasped, "Thank you," and galloped off to the bus-stop and had time to glance at the cheque. Unbelievably it was indeed for thirty-five pounds; I was stunned. I had worked for this person for seven years and she had never been renowned among her staff for her generosity. Our wage at that time was one and ninepence an hour, while people we knew in the local town were getting two and threepence, and the only reason I was still working there was that I loved the old Grange itself and when we moved further away my employer said she would pay all bus fares as she was unwilling to lose me, and I was not prepared to cycle so far.

Neither of us could know then that this apparently random act had bound me to her at a time when she would most need me. It turned out that during my stay in Cyprus several members of staff had left for various reasons, and soon after my return this poor soul had some sort of a stroke which left her almost blind and with a progressive disease which resulted in her death soon after I had repaid my debt to her.

Who says there are no hidden forces at work behind the scenes in our lives? Not I, for I have seen too many unexplained happenings; could she have had a premonition that she would have particular need of me? I recall her insistence that I go immediately, at once; not soon or next month or after Christmas, but now. I have pondered this many times since. I went into overdrive, setting all in motion. Having bought my ticket and sent a cable to Dolly and Co. saying I would be in Nicosia at 9 a.m. local time, on 7th November, I busied myself with my packing. I went to work for the last time, said goodbyes, received good wishes, and caught my bus, secure in the knowledge that all was in hand.

Arriving home I had divested myself of my coat and was about to put the kettle on, I opened the door to a knock and there to my horror stood Dolly. I was so shocked I was dumb. My mind seethed like a cauldron; something had "happened", Vin had been recalled, my holiday was off, and all my traumas had been for nothing; the hard graft, the overtime, the "making do", all for nothing. I was shattered and came round to hear Dolly's brother saying "Haven't you got the bloody kettle on yet?"

I was still in the doorway not even asking them in. Galvanised into action, I disappeared into the kitchen, determined not to show my dismay further, when I heard Dolly say "I've come to take you back with me."

Seeing my disbelief, she explained that her father had died, the funeral had been yesterday and she had postponed her return so we could travel together. This was great news and a bonus in that we could catch up on the news from both families, on the wing, so to speak.

Within half an hour I was ready for the "off". We threw the impedimenta into the car, took a fond farewell of the family and was on course for an overnight stay in London with Dolly's mum prior to our flight. I was bubbling at the thought of my first long flight, which was a pity, as long before we reached Athens I had bubbled over; but this was a minor embarrassment in a good trip.

I felt a mounting excitement as we descended at Athens. These were pre-hijacking days and we all came out of the plane and into the lounge, and that is where I first heard Greek music, with which I was so smitten that I now have a small collection of ethnic music from which ever country I find myself in.

I had imagined that, being so near the Middle East, the diversity of travellers would keep me more than interested, but in the event, one fez worn with a lounge suit and one sheik in full Arab dress struck the only foreign note, but I saw some truly beautiful faces with jet black eyes and tresses to match, and a strikingly lovely natural blonde whose eyes were darkest of all.

Over the Aegean and the Eastern Mediterranean I slept a little and felt much improved as we flew over the island. As we landed all those who had come to meet the plane could be seen standing in a wire cage, and as we crossed the tarmac people were calling and waving. We entered the customs shed and made a long queue controlled by an official who had evidently got out of bed on the wrong side that day and seemed determined to spoil everyone else's day as well. His method was to take a long cool look down the line, point his finger and snarl "You," which unfortunate creature stepped up to the trestle with all his luggage.

The magic number for the day was apparently seven, as I stood I counted the number going on between hiccups. Some people in front tried to pass the young sailor at the table only to be motioned back with a scowl and "I say when".

We had no alternative but to wait as the customs man took everything from every bag whilst the boy got more and more flustered. Finally another official appeared and opened another place and we all passed the youngster valiantly stuffing everything back into his baggage.

A boisterous welcome from Dolly's family led to great hilarity and on the way to the car Vin suddenly said, "What about the rest of your luggage?"

"I have it," I said.

"One case?" he asked, taken aback.

He had forgotten I had never been used to a car and packed accordingly. Life had been made a lot easier by the new man-made fibres, and Be and I had been careful in our choice of materials. My dresses really were uncrushable, and full-length evening dresses were seldom *de rigueur* at that time and short cocktail dresses were "in", so packing was simplified. I rolled it all tightly and on arrival shook the items out and after hanging for half an hour they were ready for wearing.

66

I had begun my Cyprus trip with a preconceived idea that the island would be a green gem set in a blue sea with a white ruffle of foam surrounding it; here, I was badly mistaken, as the overall colour was brown, but the water was indeed blue and the foam ruffle was in evidence but once away from the airport, we began to see plenty of colour.

We passed small houses covered in bougainvillaea, jasmine and passion flower, all tumbling in beautiful disarray, and geranium was everywhere. Dolly said, "Wait till the rains come. You'll really see something then." Not wishing to make early acquaintance with rain, I hoped it would not put in an appearance too soon, but Dolly was right. When the rain did arrive the result was a revelation. Overnight the brown sandy ground was clothed in glorious technicolour; lush green studded with wild flowers of every kind and colour and wild vine types rioting in every direction.

Travelling from the airport one of the unbelievable sights were gangs of women in long black skirts, dark blouses and headscarves, pushing barrows full of cement, carrying bricks and walking with heavily laden baskets on the hip. We passed several building sites with not a man in sight, but going through the villages we saw dozens of men, all looking elegant in impeccable white nylon shirts, presumably spending the money their wives were earing on the building sites.

We passed donkeys with great loads, some with a rider wielding a stick with sickening enthusiasm and often a woman trailing behind as loaded as the animal.

Someone was telling me that the locals had a little trick to minimise their misfortunes. Should a beast die it might be left out on the road after dark, in the hope that a service man would run into it, it's value being recovered from the British government. If true, it must be the only time a donkey tweaked a lion's tail.

Vin's day began at seven, which meant that some days he would be back at lunch time and we were free to go sightseeing. I discovered there were two ranges of mountains on the island, the Kyrenia range in the north and the Troodos range in the centre, both beautiful, and each quite different from the other. I went many times to Kantara Castle in the north. In fact, I was so smitten with it that if asked where I would like to go today, I always answered, "Kantara," which led, in due course, to my being known as "Kantara Kate", a soubriquet still used by Dolly and her family to this day.

One visit to Kantara resulted in a psychic experience of some interest. We were a party of eight to begin with, but during our explorations we became separated and I found myself alone at the foot of a small flight of stone steps, in a room with crumbling walls and no roof. As I looked about with interest I became aware of movement on a large scale. It seemed to be quite natural and I felt part of it. I heard horses stamping, harness jingling, and hammers on anvils. There was muted conversation as if in the next room, an odd shout and neigh, and surrounding all was a feeling of business and bustle as of a regiment on the move. I then realised I was listening intently, almost holding my breath because the movement had all but ceased and the last thing I heard was a faint snort as from a distant horse going away.

I am no stranger to 'funny feelings', premonitions and the like, but that was one of the most interesting. What had I tuned into? The Crusades? Had I heard the crusaders in the eleventh century, or the occupants of the castle years later going out to drive the Genoese forces back down the hill? I read that Prince John of Antioch had escaped capture when in Famagusta when the Genoese had occupied the city, and disguised as a cook came safely to Kantara.

The castle was still fortified in the early fifteen hundreds but soon was partly demolished and time and weather have completed the ruin. Standing at the highest pint one can see the mountains of Turkey across the narrow straits and can understand how it was so easy for the Turks to invade in 1974, but now, more than a decade on, moves are afoot to bring some semblance of normality to the disrupted lives of the inhabitants of the island. The delights of Northern Cyprus have, as a consequence of the hostilities been denied to tourists, who have missed some of the most beautiful scenery, and buildings like Hilarion and the romantic town of Kyrenia, for many years favoured by those British about to retire from service or civil life.

Packs of feral dogs roamed freely, supposedly descended from escaped hounds brought to Cyprus, it is said, by Lord Kitchener while resident on the island. Inbreeding had resulted in an ugly type of animal far removed from their ancestors; tall in the leg, thin rangy beasts, they slunk about keeping their distance, snarling and fighting among themselves.

I met most of the family friends, the first of whom turned out to be the best friend of one of my Burton upon Trent cousins. Another odd thing came to light shortly after this; conversation turned to Leicestershire and I agreed it was a lovely county. I said I had lived there in 1935 at an old Elizabethan manor house called Beau Manor. Immediately all talk ceased and everyone looked my way. "What's wrong?" I asked them. Someone said, "We all did our training at Beau Manor" and off we all went again on another conversational kaleidoscope to discover that some of the locals were known to many of us.

I would have loved to go into the Turkish quarter in Famagusta, knowing there was a great deal of craft work to be seen there, but I was advised to forego the pleasure as a precaution, due to the unrest which was never far below the surface. I then discovered a shop in town selling both Cypriot and Turkish needle-work. I wanted tray cloths and some of those I saw should have been under glass as being too exquisite to use. The Cypriot cloths were ecru coloured and the Turkish ones were highly coloured traditional designs, totally unlike each other but both very beautiful. The lady who ran the shop showed me tablecloths as big as bedspreads which had been worked by whole families of women and girls, the old women never needing spectacles to do this lovely embroidery.

The souvenir shops were full of imported carvings, animals from Kenya, cedar wood chests from Israel, tables from India, whose shell inlay tops came off their folding legs, all of which must be an indication of our shrinking world, with all the plane travel and the world's peripatetic millions. The magic of a phrase like "Toledo blade", "Astrakhan", "Apfelstrudel" and "Pizza", which once sent me off on mental journeyings, has been lost in the local High Street and Sunday markets, for now you can get everything from everywhere, everywhere else.

I seemed to be the only person walking about without a jumper or cardigan of some kind, they were all in top coats, which seemed hilarious to me. "This is winter," they said, "We're cold."

We went to Salamis, where St. Paul came ashore with St. Barnabas, when they made their epic journey to spread Christ's teachings through the rest of the known world. Standing on the old quay, waves gently lapping, I could see through the crystal waters the timber of an even more ancient jetty, perhaps the very one on to which Paul stepped ashore from the ship bringing him from his homeland.

Paul had been active against Jesus during the Teacher's lifetime, and had been among the crowd stoning St. Stephen to death for being a follower of the Messiah. Travelling to Damascus, intent on the persecution of deviants from orthodox Judaism, Paul, perhaps moved by the demeanour of the gentle St. Stephen, received a conversion, which resulted in the momentous decision to take the new teachings into the world. The undertaking was so successful that by A.D. 300 there were Christian settlements across Europe and into northern Britain.

St. Barnabas, meanwhile, had founded his monastery a short distance from Salamis and here we found a warm welcome. Monks dressed in black habits and with heavy black beards, moved quietly about as we crossed the courtyard. One great tree gave shelter from the sun and as we approached a monk rose from his seat in the shade.

"I welcome you," he said, "I am sure you are from England." We said we were indeed and he beckoned a shaven headed lad in a black cassock who was passing. The boy came quickly across the square. "Bring refreshments for our guests." then turning to us he asked "Coffee? white, black or Turkish perhaps, or there is also lemonade?"

We sat in the shadow of the tree while we waited and the monk spoke of the history of the island in general and of the monastery in particular. The monks of St. Barnabas are renowned throughout the world for their religious ikons which are in almost every country.

We enjoyed the church, white painted within, and with many examples of their pictures on the walls. There were rows of misericords used by those pursuing their devotions, each one of sufficient proportions for one person standing; however, should worship go on long enough for the suppliant to become weary, a small hinged bracket could be lowered to lean against. Too small to be sat on I felt the cure to be worse than the ailment.

We put something in the offertory box, the monk having directed our attention to it in a most courteous manner, and then as we were about to say our "goodbyes" he said in a chummy sort of way, "Do you happen to have any English sweets with you? Our young ones do love them." As he had already told us that he had been for some time at the Greek Orthodox church in Euston Road, I felt it would be an old boy who would be more interested. I rummaged about and found a roll of peppermints and one of wine gums, for which I received profuse thanks, while having a sneaking feeling that a box of Black Magic might have been more to his taste.

Salamis was so interesting that I made several trips during my eight weeks in Cyprus, drawn by the magnificence of the ruined Roman Forum of about 1000 B.C. I never cease to be amazed at the endless skills of the Romans; they were remarkable builders, masons, engineers, plumbers and architects, as witnessed by their roads, baths, aqueducts, theatres and mosaics, which are still being unearthed at intervals all over Europe and the Near East. A beautiful example of a Roman amphitheatre was found on the island in 1960 and the find was still a topic of conversation when I was there in 1964. One amateur dramatic group were inspired to do Shakespeare there and a very entertaining production it proved to be.

There was a small temple with figures of gods and goddesses around the walls, some lying prone, having fallen from their plinths, some had limbs missing and in some cases heads had rolled in the dust, leaving for posterity hundreds of photographs of British service personnel with their heads on Aphrodite's body.

One's imagination was not too stretched to people the Marble forum with sedately pacing senators engaged in an erudite conversation or discussing governmental issues of the day among the tall columns. The only occupants nowadays are lizards and snakes, none of which crossed my path.

I was taken to a citrus grove which proved a relaxing change from our frantic comings and goings, the dark green of the foliage being a foil to the luminous yellow globes within, sometimes giving the impression that the trees were dimly lit, and imparting an ethereal quality to the scene.

My last day in Cyprus was memorable for the severe storm which began as we left Famagusta for the airport. We left the house in bright sun but within ten minutes the rain came down in torrents and it was impossible to tell where the road ended and the verge began. After a few miserable kilometres we stopped to take counsel and decided to press on, although water was up to the axles and we travelled at snail's pace. We had allowed plenty of time for the journey but all the same I was late at the airport and only caught my flight by the skin of my teeth, with no time for "goodbyes" prolonged or otherwise. I heard later that my driver had only been able to start back as my plane was due in at Heathrow.

So, with the longed for trip behind me and Christmas only two weeks off, I had plenty to occupy my thoughts, interupted only by the sight of the Alps tinged delicately pink by the setting sun.

Chapter Eight

A few months after my return my lady died and changes came to my routine. Her husband sold the property and purchased a smaller one. He was close to retirement and the children from both their previous marriages were married and settled in their own establishments spread around the country. He asked me to continue to work for him and offered a taxi each way, but George and I decided against it as it was obvious that dad was less able to deal with things as he had in the past and we could see the time approaching when I must spend more and more time with him.

I was sad to leave the old house where I had worked for so many years under two owners. I had imbibed so much history while there. The oldest part of the house had been a monastery in the tenth century and the monk's cellar was a work of art. It was divided into different sections by wide archways. The floor was amazing, made of small briquettes laid in squares and herring-bone patterns. I invented excuses to go down to look at it.

The place had an aura of its own, strengthened no doubt by the antiques it contained. Some of the furniture could only be described as having been built; the refectory table was made of two massive slabs of oak placed lengthwise. On grand occasions it seated thirty guests, and was a perfect companion for the Jacobean buffet with its pewter tankards and 1604 carved into the centre door.

After a few weeks at home I began to enjoy being free of the tyranny of the bus timetable and became a dedicated gardener with George, when we began the changes that led to the garden being one of the most attractive in the village. We had many Americans coming into see Lou about birds and some of the wives took dozens of pictures and slides to take back to show their garden clubs.

Dick and Rene decided to take a chalet for their holiday that year and invited us. We were a family party of eight, and although I enjoyed the gathering, the grey sea and cool winds of Hayling Island lost any charms they might have had when compared to Paphos and Kyrenia.

About two years after my time in Cyprus, Dolly and I decided to try a package tour to Rudesheim which proved a disaster, as I was ill from start to finish. We had a long series of mishaps which began with a party of five missing their train from Victoria, which delayed us for over two hours. We were all fed up by the time they arrived, in a chauffeur driven car provided by the tour company and to add insult to injury they all went aboard first.

Without doubt this was the worst journey I ever experienced and remained so for twenty years. I believe this whole episode had a psychological base started in the airport lounge when the group were late. This fact got folk mad knowing that their holiday time was being frittered away, and then when they did arrive in a VIP haze, the latecomers said brightly, "Ever so sorry, we overslept." Several people made rude remarks in loud voices such as "We could all have done the same and arrived in a Daimler," and "They can have foreign holidays and can't afford an alarm clock."

We stowed all our gear and waited for the "off" which never came. Apologies from our captain for the delay and again for the present one due to a slight technical problem. In ten minutes our engines sprang into life and we were away. Or were we? Obviously not, as we reached the main runway our pilot crackled his way through another "Sorry, we must return to the building. We have an engine fault."

As we glided to a halt two men with a ladder appeared: they propped it up against our engine, poked about a bit here and there, did a thumbs up towards the plane, and once again the engines began to purr.

By now rain was coming down in sheets and I had availed myself of the services of the stewardess to dispose of my used bag although we had not yet left the ground. Lying back in my seat I could see the wing and saw a movement. "Did you see that?" I asked Dolly.

"No,"she said, "What was it?"

"I'm sure I saw a flash" I replied and as I spoke we both saw a tongue of flame leap above the wing. At the same moment the pilot's voice went through his routine once again, apologies, technical problem, return to airport buildings, etc. etc.

Another half-hour delay and then we were really off; and people who had been very quiet during the trauma began to relax and conversation began to hum. Twenty minutes into the flight the captain came through again saying chattily "Please fasten your seat belts. We are entering a period of turbulence, but I am sure it will be of short duration."

Well, how wrong can you be? By now we had thunder and lightning, a strong wind coming from the side, and when we flew out of that we were bombarded with very large hailstones. Many of the passengers were ill and even Dolly felt queasy, so she had a brandy to "settle" her stomach. Well, it may have done wonders for her stomach, but the effect her brandy had on mine was nobody's business. The combined affluvia of the alcohol and her Chanel did me no good at all and I was thankful to feel the plane coming in at Luxembourg. In spite of all the miseries I never felt sorry I had come on this trip and was eager to get on to the next stage.

A coach awaited our arrival but there was another delay while everyone rushed to the toilets to tidy up after such an awful flight. Once aboard our driver introduced himself saying he would be with us for the duration of our stay, but that owing to our very late arrival we had missed the ferry across the Rhine and as it was now closed we must make a much longer journey in order to cross by bridge. Consequently dinner at the hotel would be finished, but refreshments would be awaiting our arrival. In the event all one really needed was a cup of tea, a sandwich and bed.

However, the next day with good humour restored, we boarded the coach for a local tour, some vineyards and then to a world famous brandy distillery. The weather was good, the scenery beautiful, and I was going to enjoy the break although I was not back to normal by any means, so I favoured my innards and ate sparingly. We found ourselves sharing a table with a Surrey farmer and his family and we got on so well that we ate together for the rest of the holiday. The two lads, aged seventeen and eighteen, could never get enough to fill them so I accepted all that the waiter offered and passed the surplus to a good home.

Being the only teetotaller on this trip I found myself to be an object of curiosity and from time to time people tried to buy me drinks of various kinds. Some thought I was too shy to order, and I think one thought I made an excuse because I could hardly afford to buy. In vain did Dolly protest that I never drank alcohol. Among the party was a man from Bristol travelling alone, and he seemed desperate to be bosom chums with everyone, full of tales about the pop groups he managed.

We all shared a long table in a beer cellar and after a discussion with the traditionally costumed waitress I had ordered a very saintly drink, St. Batholomew's wine or St. Benedict's ale and I had this good looking bottle in front of me while listening to the band. We were all laughing and singing when we could join in, when the chap from Bristol, who had sampled everything the waitress had suggested up to then, called for a double brandy. The drink appeared smartly for which my friend paid, then he pushed it in front of me not seeing he had spilled some, perhaps he could hardly see the table either at that stage.

"There you are." he said. "We know you're the life and soul without it. Let's see what you're like with it!"

The people on either side and opposite were staring and my face was feeling like a stop traffic light, and I heard myself say "Whatever I'd be like with a double, you would be unlikely to benefit." I moved the glass to my left and placed it before him, "Have this on me," I said.

I am not at my best when embarrassed, but I exercised restraint and did not push him off his seat; someone tittered as the band began again, my friend took out his handkerchief mopped his brow and left the table muttering something about air. Somebody called out, "If you had played your cards right you could have ended up with your own group," which caused a few smiles.

The brandy distillery was a wonderful sight. From the time we entered the building we were on closed circuit TV. Pristine white walls was the background to enormous copper vats and miles of polished brass pipes winking in all directions. A guide explained all the processes as we went along and we finally arrived in a small bar where we were to receive a sample of the product.

The place was crowded as we had caught up with another tour, and not wishing to cause any more schemozzle over my peculiar drinking habits I moved away from the bar area and came face to face with the courier of the other party, who said, "Hello. What are you doing here? You don't drink, or are you reformed?" He had been our courier in Holland, and remembered us at once. Now after that I don't know if I am renowned, famous or notorious.

The best part for me was the cruise down the Rhine. The great river, a thousand miles long, flows for several miles in a deep gorge, the cliffs rising high on either side between Boppard where we boarded and Rudesheim where we went ashore.

We were blest with a soft balmy day, which together with

the gliding motion of the boat clothed the whole thing in a magical haze, emphasised by the unobtrusive background music. The guide was informative, with a fund of historical anecdotes and a comical delivery.

Robber barons had built their castles on mountain tops in order to see the next craft to be plundered approaching their territory, two being Castel Maus and Castel Katz, the former being named in a derisory manner by the brigand who lived in the latter, presumably an early example of psychological advantage.

The Rhine has always been a danger to shipping and work goes on to make it safer; the Lorelie Rock has for centuries been a hazard to seamen who, legend says, were lured to their death by the seductive singing of the beautiful Siren who inhabited this vertical rock.

Roman history abounds in these parts, including several spas with healing properties, and one interesting item about which I was told but had no time to see. There is a firm based in Mainz which has sixty cellars on many levels which were used by the Romans and in all probability were built by them.

I disembarked with the feeling that one day I would travel the entire length of the Rhine from Rotterdam to Switzerland, but this has not yet come to pass, although I live in hope. meantime I met a couple who were very taken with the area and were currently making their arrangements to travel the Rhine by car, down on one bank and back on the other side, which sounded very satisfying to me.

The next jaunt was to Schaesberg in Holland, where Janet and her family had been living for the past two years; the house was not large enough for all our gang, but the problem was solved by George and I sleeping at Janet's house and Dolly, Vin and Reg putting up in a nearby hotel. We made forays into the German forests, sometimes we holiday-makers only, and sometimes when Rick was off duty we would all go in a family party.

He took us twice to Aachen, known in the first war as Aix-la-Chappelle and now well known as the venue for the International Horse Show, but to we holiday-makers, Aachen is remembered for the restaurant in the town centre.

The place was filled with wrought iron and polished wood and had a marvellous atmosphere. The speciality of the house at that time was mussels, which came to the table in large deep plates accompanied by clouds of steam. Each table had its own small beer barrel in a cradle and when necessary these were refilled from an enormous cask lifted up from the cellar on chains. Each time a new cask came up to floor level a loud bell rang; it is not difficult to imagine the pandemonium between ordinary conversation, orders to the waiting staff, the rattle of the chains as the next barrel began its ascent and the cheers of the clientele as the cask came into view, followed by the triumphant clang of the bell. Need I say, having made two visits, we are all ready to go there again, as a more hilarious night out would be hard to find, unless time has changed things.

We had one miserable incident during a forest drive one day. The weather was extremely hot, although it was late in September, and Vin decided to call in at the next inn we came to for a cold drink. Turning a bend in the road we came to a clearing, in the middle of which stood the prettiest little hostelry one could find in a day's march. Troughs and tubs stood around, among standard fuchias, roses and geraniums, giving the whole scene a chocolate-box look.

Pulling up in the parking area, we entered the quaint old building, peering a little after the bright sun outdoors. Vin went to the bar to order for us, ending his request with the words, "Will you accept sterling?"

The girl behind the bar, arms akimbo, said in a loud offensive manner, "Sterling? Wass ist das sterling?"

A raucous cheer went up from an alcove we had not previously seen. Several locals were drinking at the table and one got to his feet and began to slouch towards Vin.

Dolly rose from her seat as the other men began to cat call. Reg and I began to walk towards Vin who was carrying the tray when cries of "Nein, nein," were heard, followed by a small scuffle as the belligerent one was dragged back to his seat by his best mate. When we reached our table we found two elderly men talking to Dolly. It seemed they started forward to remonstrate with the locals, but seeing it about to fizzle out had then apologised to her for the uncouth behaviour of their fellow countrymen. It appeared they were lifelong friends who had served in the Wehrmacht, had been together on the Russian front and in France and were finally captured in Italy by the British, coming to a quiet backwater on an English farm.

They told us they had found nothing but kindness from all they had met in Britain and had maintained yearly contact, and now the English were coming to them on holiday and their families travelled to England in the same way.

We parted with a handshake and were surprised to find the alcove empty. We wondered if we would meet trouble outside, but all was well and we were able to enjoy the remainder of our day before crossing the border back into Holland.

Chapter Nine

In 1968 we had a visit from Lou's son, Vlado, who had been reared by Lou's mother. Although there had been plenty of correspondence through the years, father and son had not met for twenty-six years.

Photos came quite often and these were the only means they each had of recognising the other, so on the day of arrival, waiting for the boat train from Dover to pull in, Lou was very nervous about the forthcoming meeting. We stood one on each side of the barrier in order not to miss the traveller, and as people began to stream through in droves I though we should need to wait till the platform was empty and then see who was left; but we saw him together, head and shoulders above all the rest. We had been concentrating on a face, with no thought of height or girth. This man was very big and made his father look small.

I was official photographer for the occasion but no pictures of the meeting were taken. The two were in floods of tears and it was some time before they composed themselves enough for Lou to remember I was there at all. I had made myself as inconspicuous as possible during these emotional moments and was at the bookstall when I eventually had a good look at the new member of our family.

Of course, we were unable to talk together, as Vlado had no English and I had no Croat, so Lou had to interpret, which was fairly awkward at first as for the previous twenty-four years he had thought and spoken only in English and for the two years before that he had thought and spoken only in German. This was because the Germans had taken all the young men from their Yugoslav villages to be conscripts in the German army. In the course of events, Lou had been picked up in Italy by the British who then gave him a reserved passage to England on the Queen Mary, then being used as a troopship.

Unknown to Vlado, we had also arranged for Lou's sister, Evka, a widow, living in Czechoslavkia, to come for the first time to see her young brother in England. As things worked out, Vlado was with us for one week then Evka was here with Vlado for one week. He then went home and she was here for a further week alone. When Lou said that his aunt was coming Vlado was very pleased because their meetings were few and far between.

We were all going to Heathrow to meet the Czech plane and were actually locking the door when the phone rang. I answered the call and a man asked for Lou. I asked if I could give a message as he was getting the car out before driving to Heathrow to meet his sister. "Yes", he said, "that is what I am calling about. We are already at Heathrow and I sat with Mrs Brimova from Prague, and she is worried that her brother will not know where she is."

"That is very kind of you." I said. "What is she doing now?"

"I got her a cup of coffee," he said, and sat her down where she can see me on the phone. What shall I tell her?"

"Tell her to stay where she is and we shall be there in just over an hour," I told him. I thanked him for his kindness and genuine concern for his fellow-traveller and wished we could have met him to really convey our appreciation. Evka later told me he was a British business man based in Prague, spoke the language fluently and they had been able to chat all the way.

We saw her at once as we entered the terminal, standing by a pillar, luggage at her feet, scanning the crowds. Again I had the camera, and this time I got a good shot. Vlado had moved away from Lou, who walked directly to Evka. George and I stood where we had entered and as luck had it there was a long clear space between us and them. While Lou and his sister were greeting each other, Vlado had come from behind and as Lou picked up the baggage and turned towards us, listening to Evka's animated chat, Vlado fell in to step on Evka's other side.

They had paced several yards before she realised someone was there, she glanced sideways and dismissed the man's feet as just another passenger and turned back to resume her conversation with Lou. A few more yards and those feet were still there keeping pace with hers. She took another sidelong glance and then looked straight ahead, but then decided to have a proper look. Naturally, for a few seconds she was dumbfounded but soon regained her ebullience and was delighted to take part in a family reunion.

She and I could talk all day by signs, acting a word or drawing a sketch, but we really spoke the same language in the garden. She is a garden lunatic, as I am, and we went round the garden every day and soon knew which plants or not grew in her garden, with me making my teeth chatter to show her that I could not grow oleanders as it is too cold and she flinging her arms wide to indicate carnations growing all over at home and then making exaggerated sniffs in order to comment on the beautiful perfume. We sometimes needed to have several attempts at the Latin names to allow for the difference in pronunciation, but on the whole we did well.

We had a family gathering while the Yugoslavs were with us, to enable our family and friends to meet Lou's people and it was hard going for Lou, who was not sure which language he was in at any given moment. Sometimes Evka would go next door into Lou's house for forty winks, or to look at his photos, or just for a quiet few moments. Elizabeth was always ready to have a stab at talking to the guests although she had none of their language and one time I was aware she was not among the company. Shortly after she came in and I asked where she had been.

In Lou's talking to Mrs Evka," she said..

I said, "Crikey, what about?"

"Dressmaking," said Be, "She can't stand needlework. It makes her tear her hair out."

"How on earth did you find that out," I asked, "What's Croat for tearing your hair out?"

"No idea," she said "Mrs Evka went through the motions of sewing, and then took hold of a handful of hair on top of her head, made a face and shook the hair about. It seemed to be the only conclusion to come to." Later we asked Lou to translate and sure enough that is what she had said.

Vlado learned to play darts whilst with us and one day he gave George a thrashing. He was so crazy about the game that George sent him home with a dartboard and darts so that he could teach his friends.

We needed to go to the travel agents to check on Evka's return journey because while she was in England the Russians had driven their tanks in to Prague to do away with the government of Mr. Dubchek. Lou asked her to stay with us but the thought of her family and the idea that she may never see them again brought a tearful refusal.

The day we decided to see about the ticket she said she would stay and see to the meal. We had stew and dumplings and it was arranged that she would put the dumplings in to be ready for our return. When we arrived she was in a worried state because the dumplings kept coming up so she was trying to hold them down with a wooden spoon. The explanation, of course, was that they never use self-raising flour; when they need something to be light they use yeast or eggs.

Evka taught me to make strudel and I was surprised to find it bore very little relation to what is called strudel in shops. I thought apple was the only filling for strudel but then I found that walnuts were widely used, also cheese made a good flavour and I now make it for all our family gatherings by request. I have one reservation about it; our kitchen work-tops are so small these days that I have to pull the paste out on my dining-table, it being the only area large enough. As soon as the dish is put in the oven the floured cloth gets shaken in the garden and the cleaner has to go over the carpet, making extra work. A real farmhouse kitchen table is the ideal thing for the job.

Both Evka and Vlado asked us to visit them in due course, and as money was not too plentiful, we started planning almost at once to make the journey in 1971.

However, planning is one thing and getting said plan off the ground quite another. It so happened that the next year 1970, redundancy notices went out and George was one of those to go. He was upset, but I quietly cheered, because he often went to work when he should have stayed home. The big problem was how to keep him happy at home? We had a big garden and went in for a greater variety of vegetables and took more interest in fruit growing.

He was doing a DIY job about three days before his last day at work, when he fell from a step-ladder and broke some ribs, in the event, this was a considerable help in getting over the transition between work and dole, although one would hesitate to recommend broken ribs as a remedy for anything.

Within a week we heard that Lou also was to be redundant in January '71, so there we were with two mopey folk at home. My dad had died a couple of years before and his cottage had come to me, and after doing it up I had let it to an American family, but it was all too recent to have been a profit to us. I went to collect the rent to hear that the Americans had been recalled to the States and would be gone in a very short time.

When I got home Lou was grumbling to George that his birdseed supplier was closing and developing their business about fifteen miles away. This also affected me because I bought our pet foods at the same shop, so I was not pleased either. Then a little light began to flash in my brain-box, and I really began to think.

I found that each flash illuminated dad's cottage, and the germ that was writhing about in my head frightened the life out of me, but I knew with one of my 'funny' feelings that opportunity was knocking.

The redundancy squad were in front of the television smoking themselves silly and commiserating with each other when I dropped my bombshell. "We should open a shop," I said.

One said "How" and the other said "What with?"

Before I could reply one said "What sort of a shop?" and the other, "We don't know anything about business."

"At the moment it's just an idea, but I'm working on it," I said. I argued that the shop which was due to close would leave a gap in our local High Street, as it was the only pet shop in the town. I pointed out that Lou already had a lot of contacts in the pet trade from disposing of a few birds over the years, and that common sense was a great help in a crisis, and I had plenty of that. Someone kept saying "money" so I said, "Imagine if I could magic dad's cottage into a shop."

Cutting a long story short, I saw the estate agent to ask first if there was a small shop property to rent. There were one or two, one which was miles too big and whose rates bill was astronomical, and the other was too far from the main shopping street to attract any customers. The outcome was that if anything turned up they would ring me.

My next visit to the office was quite exciting. A property had arrived on their desk and they felt it would suit our purpose. Would I like to see it? The shop had been a cottage, two up and two down, but when the last occupant had died her family decided to convert it into a small shop in order to realise a better price. It was just right for size, the only criticism was that it was down a side street off the main shopping area, but a small plus were the town toilets at the far end of this little lane, as I discovered when I noticed a steady flow of people who went by and then a few minutes later came back. This fact was very useful years later when we had started a small garden department and found that holiday-makers stop in the town *en route* to the north for a meal and toilets.

Passing the shop we have heard them say, "We'll look in there going back." They would come in and say how glad they were that we had plants for sale as they had forgotten a present for Auntie Mary, or they would take a chew bone for Fido who had stayed with grandma. In fact, we had a Scottish family and some people from Yorkshire who came year after year and we got to know them quite well.

We discussed the whole idea at great length on the basis that George would serve in the shop, Lou would fetch and carry and do the customer deliveries, and I would stay home and do the ordering and keep the books. The estate agent was glad to have a quick decision and asked if we would need a mortgage. I told him there was a freehold cottage for sale, which pleased him and within six weeks we were signing the papers and dad's cottage had been magicked into a shop.

Such a busy time ensued, making the shop fittings, seeing the council, arranging insurance, going to wholesalers, that any thought of the holiday went by the board. George built shelves and a counter in the shop and Lou got on with his birdcages and aviaries in the yard at the side.

Then George had one of his bad illnesses and it became obvious that he would never be able to be in the shop full-time as we had hoped. So we opened for business on 6th June 1971 and I went daily for the first six months and thereafter Lou managed the business alone. Fortunes were not made but it gave us all an interest at a time when it would have been easy to get demoralised, although we had a few unexpected matters to deal with, like decimalisation, and VAT among them.

By now Lou's family were asking for dates, and I looked at the piles of tinned food and packet goods I had stashed away against the holiday, at the gas cooker, lantern and sleeping-bags, and thought how sad it was that so many people were due to be disappointed, and made a mental note to remind Lou to tell his family the trip was shelved for some time to come.

Chapter Ten

In due course the man from the Pru arrived for his monthly collection; we always had a cup of coffee together and put the world to rights, but this day he was rather quiet, but managed to ask about George and how the shop was doing. I remarked that he was a bit subdued to which he agreed and said he was to retire at the end of the month and this was the last time he would be coming to me. I commiserated with him saying we knew only too well the misery of a routine coming to a stop after so many years.

He then said he and his wife had thought of the possibility of running a small business here and there while the proprietors took their holidays, or were sick. I was mesmerised.

"What's wrong?" He said.

"Nothing," I said "Everything's right. You have been sent to me today. Will you accept your first shop job?"

It was his turn to be mesmerised. "What do you mean?" he asked. I explained our dilemma as to the holiday and how our plans had been frustrated. He was delighted, so we pored over the calendar to get our dates right, as he and his wife were going on holiday immediately following his last day at work, and the bargain was struck. They would manage the shop for three weeks while we all went to Yugoslavia for the long desired holiday.

The even tenor of George's way was undisturbed and Lou really thought it was a joke to begin with, but eventually they both got caught up in the preparations, and the letter went off to the family that we would be there in due course.

My Uncle Jim and his wife, Connie, volunteered to live at our place to look after dogs, cats and birds, while we were away and suddenly all was in train for the great exodus. A lot of planning had been done, with a list of needs for each of the weeks we were to be away handed to our friends from the Pru, and enough signed cheques to pay the suppliers as our orders were delivered. The bank was advised that someone else would be in charge, we handed over the keys and we were off.

The first three weeks in September had been chosen as Lou said the weather was then still hot in Yugoslavia, but we said rude words when we actually got there and found they were having the coldest, wettest September they'd had for years. But we had a few miles to go before we discovered that.

Our party consisted of Lou, George and myself, Elizabeth, her husband and two children, and Colin who had worked with George. Four of the party were to do the driving between them and George and I were to be the canteen staff.

We left England on Thursday morning in beautiful weather, and crossed the Channel on a calm sea. Our drivers had decided to drive through the night, so we set course for Strasbourg and only stopped for the usual reasons. About 2.00 a.m. we stopped for tea and had just driven through a small French village, pulling up on the grass verge beside a stone barn. George and I got out to do our stuff quietly as the boys were asleep in the back. The kettle was not yet humming when we heard a small noise. Thinking we had imagined it, we waited for the kettle and heard it again. A small chinking sound "What the hell's that?" George said.

"It sounds like money." Who the devil would be counting money in the middle of nowhere at this time of night?" I said.

We passed the mugs into the van, speaking in whispers. Everyone got out to listen, holding their breath when suddenly there was a long low "moo-o-o" and the clink of chain as a cow got to her feet inside the barn. We all heaved a sigh of relief and then had a good laugh at ourselves, all coming from the country and not even thinking cows could have been in a barn.

We needed to stop for fresh milk and bread at the earliest opportunity, which was about six o'clock in the morning. I was not looking forward to it as I only had school French and I had never spoken any since leaving school, but fortune favours the brave, and when I entered the village shop several housewives were there buying their croissants for breakfast, so I had time to listen to them and rehearse my own items before my turn came.

I was very surprised to find I was able to make a passable job of it and bought more things than I had intended, on the strength of my new found confidence, not the least pleasure was the fact that I had staggered my daughter.

We traversed Strasbourg a couple of times before hitting the Munich exit and found beautiful wooded areas on our way. By common consent we concluded that we would camp either before Munich or after, wherever a campsite showed itself, as we had been travelling so long. A site notice appeared and we followed the signs off the autobahn to a pretty hollow surrounded by tall pines, and only one tent in evidence.

While George filled the kettle and got the stove going, I booked us in and the others got the tent up. Well, that is to say, they wanted to pitch the tent; what stopped them was the rocky ground, as they moved from place to place trying to find enough soil to take a tent-peg.

Eventually, two bent pegs later, we understood the significance of the empty site, and I wondered how many other campers had turned in so gleefully as we, at the thought of a site to themselves.

As the meal neared completion, we decided to eat first, just as the occupant of the other tent arrived, and said, "Have you had trouble finding a spot?" We said we had and he pointed to a place saying, "It's not bad there." And in no time at all we were fixed up and hitting the hay in anticipation of an early start in the morning.

George and I were up first, organising breakfast, when our neighbour appeared. He began by telling us he had been walking Scandinavia for three months and had been offered a lift by a Danish truck driver and felt it was too good an opportunity to miss. His problem was that now he had got as far as Munich he had to look to getting back to England as his money was running low.

As he was talking I had been passing bacon and egg as each of our party was ready and passed him one just before he got to the bit about money shortage, so he was able to take it and I was able to give it without embarrassment on either side; he ate it with relish and said it would see him a mile or two further on the way to London.

On to Vienna and we were looking for toilets, so parking in a side-street, we followed signs which led us to a very important road with four lanes in each direction, divided by islands, on one of which the toilets were situated. At that moment the lanes we needed to cross were empty and we wondered why there was a knot of people waiting to cross at the corner.

We gathered ourselves into a group and started across and immediately all hell was let loose. Whistles shrilled, people shouted and when we looked around at the hubbub there was a policeman alternately waving and blowing and looking as if he would have apoplexy at any minute. A solitary car arrived at the intersection, which he flagged down with great ceremony, waving us all across, wagging his finger and showing his whistle as we passed close to his rostrum.

Having got over that hurdle without dire consequences we advanced on the toilets. They had an entrance at each end, one was marked Herrren to the left and the one to the right said Frauen. We divided our forces, Elizabeth and I going to the right and our menfolk to the left, out of our sight until we were half-way down the stairs to the Ladies and suddenly there we were all meeting at the bottom.

Green, gold and white was the first impression given by green and white tiles, criss-crossed by miles of copper and brass pipe winking in the electric light. There was a bamboo table, covered by a hand-made lace tablecloth, standing before an antique gilt mirror which looked as if it might have come from the Royal Palace, and on the table a fat-bellied old art pot containing an over-large aspidistra, whose leaves shone in unison with all the other polished surfaces.

There was no discernable receptacle for money in view, and it became obvious that we were to give the money to the custodian, who looked as if her normal wear should have been a black uniform, boots, whip and a large Alsatian dog.

Someone proffered money and she let forth a stream of invective, only a few words of which I could pick out, while she ferreted about in cavernous pockets for change, and we supposed our crime to be that we had the wrong coins. Martin and Barry were fascinated by this gorgon and stood before her, looking up into her face as though entranced, which made it difficult to maintain sobriety while she read the riot act, but when we were all settled we retreated up our separate staircases, her raucous voice becoming fainter as we reached the upper level.

The plan was to go into Czechoslovakia to Lou's sister Evka, and stay a few days to meet her family, consisting of a son and daughter and their spouses and children, so we lost no time in Vienna, but made for the border in quick time.

The route ran alongside the railway which sometimes disappeared into a tunnel, but as soon as we noticed the line had gone it reappeared beside us, which was very interesting to two small boys, and then along came a train. The driver blew his whistle and we all waved until they went into the next tunnel and then forgot about him, but in a few minutes the train was there again, this time behind us and whistling furiously until we waved again, and these manoeuvres were repeated again and again for miles and miles. The next time we saw them they were in front with both driver and fireman leaning out of the cab waving their caps. Those two men could not have known how much pleasure they gave to all of us, not only the two little boys, whose sharpest memory of that holiday is the train.

Some miles later we saw the train for the last time. We crossed the border into Czechoslovakia, and were wondering what sort of reception we would get. All our papers were in order as far as we were aware, but we had heard of some odd business behind the iron curtain.

The guards who came out to inspect our passports were friendly, but had little English and none of us spoke Czech. The first man said to his mate, "British", and was for waving us on, but a third man with some authority came out of the post giving some sort of order and we all had to get out of the van while the officials inspected the engine compartment and turned over our belongings. We were than ushered into the office where our papers were scrutinised and our Czech money counted. Foreigners were not allowed into the country without a specific sum of money per person, including children, and every penny of that sum had to be spent in the country, if you had any change left it was to be confiscated at the border on the way out. I had been told of this at the Czech embassy when our arrangements had been made, but not that we would be unable to bring any of it out, and at the time I felt the whole business to be very unfair as a sort of hidden tax, but thinking of it later I realised it was their Government's way of getting western currency into the country.

In the event, Evka was the one to benefit; before leaving we all turned our Czech money out on her kitchen table and in her next letter to Lou she told him we had left more than enough for her next trip to England one way, but in fact she was never to come to the west again as the rules were changed and the ordinary Czech people were not allowed exit papers. We resigned ourselves to never seeing her in England again, but ten years later when we went to Lou's home village, she was able to travel there for the family reunion.

We never arrived anywhere in daylight on this trip and were forced to knock on several doors to find our bearings. The people at one house shouted a lot of words, among which we heard "ENGLESKI" and then the whole family trooped out, obviously pleased to meet us. They kissed us all and passed Martin and Barry from one to another to be cuddled and kissed until every one had had his turn, then they were returned to the bosom of the family and we were given directions to Evka's home. Arriving there the reception ceremony was repeated and we found the English handshake was relegated to the end of affairs, so we English resigned ourselves to these funny foreign customs and soon found ourselves adopting the "one on each cheek and one in the middle" kiss, like everybody else.

Before we drew breath the bottles were out and they were all laughing and crying, including several neighbours who had got beached in the tide of people, so I made tea for myself and the boys while Be unpacked what was needed for the night.

Evka had put Be and the boys and me in her room and all the men in the bigger room. By the time we had sorted ourselves out there was a meal on the table. There was hot sausage in a liquor, a great deal of bread, cucumber, tomatoes and peppers. It was an unusual meal, but very welcome and enjoyable. Apart from the first meal, all others began with an enormous tureen of soup, but we were unable to give a definite time of arrival so soup was not on the menu.

Naturally it was not long before my unfriendly habits were in the spotlight, both Lou and Evka trying to explain my non-alcoholic life. They were asked, "Is she sick?" because tea is used only in illness, as a herbal remedy in fact. It was quite difficult for the Czechs to get the hang of it, and when I made tea for us and offered it to them they refused the first few times, laughing at the very idea, but later seeing that George, David and Colin drank it without any ill effects, first one and then another tried it and soon we were including whoever was there at the time.

Chapter Eleven

We were all glad to get to bed and soon relaxed in the knowledge that we could lie in for a while in the morning, but it seemed no sooner had we fallen asleep than we were wakened by a cacophony of sound. Well, if you are not expecting a military band at 4.00a.m., then cacophony is the only description possible. Before we had time to assimilate the idea of martial music, a voice came over the loud speakers, with more music in the intervals. It was our first cultural shock.

We discovered each day began in this way with the disembodied voice telling the villagers their jobs for the day. "Mrs Brown to the potato fields, Mrs Smith to the shop, Mr. Smith to the farm."

There is no private business, everything is state owned, and every one works for the community. So someone would deliver the potatoes round the village, another would deliver wood, each one having an allowance of everything. Some worked at the farm or with the sheep, others on the buildings and in the vineyards.

When we ventured out after breakfast we could see the public-address system attached to every telegraph pole and I made a mental note to appreciate our freedoms at home.

Evka had obtained permission for us to see a collective farm, and I enjoyed it very much. I had been in a farming environment for twenty years and had seen the industry in different counties at home but had rarely seen custom-built farm buildings, and the cow shed was the Hilton among them.

They had an ingenious way of cleaning out the shed by way of some low slung chains. Outside the shed at one end a worker cranked a handle, and all these chains moved across the cow stall, and behold the muck was all in a central gully and strong water jets swilling the floor; a large blade was pulled along the gully and in no time the place was as clean as a whistle, and not a muck fork in sight. All the muck, solid and liquid, was pulled through the wall at the end of the barn into a huge pit and from there it was taken out and spread over the fields.

We were taken to an apricot and peach farm where wine and liqueurs were made from their own produce. The cellars were quite fantastic, enormous caverns filled with hundreds of barrels. The manager was one of those folk immersed in his subject and was able to put across his facts in such a way that you had no idea that you were learning.

He was full of hectares, tonnes and litres, which led us up to a wine tasting. We were all given a small glass with the heraldic device of the cellar on it and we went from cask to cask for a taste of each vintage. I managed to circulate discreetly away from the man with the siphon, but then someone remembered me and there was a halt in the proceedings, while it was explained that I was quite alright really but had this funny way of going on. The manager's mouth dropped open; never before had this happened to him. People came hundreds of kilometres to taste his wines, which were the most beautiful wines in the whole country. He was desolated and cut to the heart, but if that was the situation then alas, he had played his part and to show that there was no ill feeling I could keep my little glass as a momento.

Martin and Barry had a wonderful time and seemed to be up front at every barrel. When we came to the exit the manager made a little speech, in which of course he said that although he was extremely happy to welcome his first English party, we were in fact the only group who had left the premises under their own steam; I think he felt it to be a slur on his capabilities, but as we drove away I noticed he had a water-melon smile and was waving like mad so maybe he was not quite so devastated as he would have liked us to believe.

The next day Evka's son Jaco, drove us to the local town, Brno, where an hilarious incident took place. Jaco parked the bus off the market square, and we wandered among the stalls where our invasion created something of a stir on account of all the different languages involved. If the Engleski wanted to ask anything then they asked Lou in English, who then asked Evka in Croat, who then spoke to her son in Croat and he then spoke to the stall holder in Czech. In the end all the people in the market were smiling and waving. Although it was lovely that they were all so friendly, we were quite pleased when it was time to go back to the bus.

George and I got in first and were just settling down when we heard a bit of commotion. I looked through the window and saw a strange man kissing my daughter's hand; in fact the picture presented was reminiscent of an historical tableau. Elizabeth with her arm outstretched and this man in a courtly posture bending over it and in his hand a small posy of flowers.

George said, "What does he think he's at then?" in the manner of one not keen on some foreign customs. "Must be a friend of Jaco's," I said, as the man moved away pushing his bike, face wreathed in smiles, and explaining to bystanders with much gesticulation. They looked towards the bus as if checking the man's story, but by then we were all aboard, Colin with a broad grin, Be with a red face, but laughing with Jaco, and David's face very dark, as you would expect from an Englishman whose wife had just shown him up in the street.

It turned out that Jaco who had a sharp sense of humour, had been walking with Be to the vehicle when the man with the bike stopped him, saying it was marvellous to see him and what a good game that was last week. As the man continued speaking Jaco realised he had been mistaken for a local footballer; he made no denial and then the fellow said, "And this is your beautiful wife?" Before Jaco could confirm or deny off he went into his courtly routine, ending by presenting the flowers to Be. I hoped it was not his his wife's birthday, or perhaps he nipped round the corner to replace his posy before going home, but whatever the circumstances, Be's day had been made.

On the following day we all went to Evka's daughter, Steffi, who worked at the old people's home. I never quite got the hang of this place, because in every home we visited there were one or two old people living with the family; either the husband's or wife's parents, or an aged grandmother, so perhaps the homes were for old people who had no families at all.

The Engleskis had been invited to a recital in the home given by some local school children, but in the event, George and I stayed outside in the bus, as he was having one of his bad times; so we took a slow stroll round the grounds and then sat in the bus and he had a nap. Be enjoyed the visit and the old folk made a fuss of Martin and Barry, but Colin, who at twenty was the youngest of the adults, made us laugh when he said, "They won't believe me when I go home and say I went to Yugoslavia to an old folk's home."

Back at Steffi's house there was a big family gathering, where we met Olin's parents, who lived with the family, and Olin and Steffi's two girls, Olina and Arlenka, and their son. The table groaned under the great bowl of soup, followed by chicken, salami of various kinds, large quantities of cucumber, tomatoes, gherkins and heaps of bread, real bread.

As ever, there was plenty of Slivovica, Kruskavac, and in deference to the Engleski, tiny cups of coffee, black, thick and very sweet.

One more treat was in store for us, when Jaco took us for lunch to a famous hunting-lodge in the mountains. In the far past it had been a private house, with an army of servants. Six enormous cannon were trained on each approach road in the valley and the place gave an impression of total impregnability, should such a need arise.

Wild boar were the quarry of the hunting fraternity using the lodge, and some types of deer, but the wolves and bear had long since departed from the area. In recent years the lodge was used as reward for work well done in government departments, and as a hospitality perk as well as being used by the public. I was sorry that no one was able to tell me the history of the castle.

The next day a treat was in store for Lou; a neighbour bred budgies and sent a message that we were all to go to his house to see his collection. We arrived *en masse* to find a modest house with a small zoo at the back. The yard was full of cages, avaries and hutches. There were parrots, finches and doves, and all kinds of small mammals, including several sorts of rabbits; these were for show as well as for the table and the owner was proud of the types uncommon in his country.

We did our packing ready to leave and then the fun began. First one would come with a gift and then another and another until we were snowed under. There were drinking glasses, ornaments, carved boxes, a cut glass fruit set, bottles of drink, and salamis by the yard. When we left the village several groups were at their gates to see us go with a great plastic-covered package ballooning on the roof of the mini-bus.

Our route was the one we had travelled from Vienna so we turned our noses towards the border and into Austria. Once again the guards flagged us down and the procedure went ahead as before, with the addition of the voluminous package on the roof. Wide smiles from the soldiers at the mass and variety of our booty and one patted his pocket and shook it to indicate that we had spent all our money.

Again we were shepherded into the office where we were

checked against our passports and another man checked we indeed had no Czech money left, then we were ushered out of the office and were soon on our way to Yugoslavia.

As we drove, we discussed the visit and thought what a funny old life it is that can make whole nations leave their homelands for new lives in strange places; had Lou's forebears not emigrated from Germany during the time of the Austro-Hungarian Empire, he might have been a full blown Nazi, instead of a victim of the German forces. As it is his family have a variety of languages between them, including Rumanian, German, Czech, Russian and English, all of which were forced on them by circumstances and not a school curriculum.

We crossed the border at Maribor having skirted Vienna and Graz and decided to press on to Lou's home village instead of camping the night, so with this in mind, Colin made the best of the, by now, awful roads, almost empty of traffic. Coming to a large village, we turned a corner and there was a policeman in the middle of the road holding a small sign up in the air which said, "STOP".

He moved to Colin's window and seemed to say a great deal in a short time. Lou was asleep in the back so we woke him up to deal with the problem. It turned out to be an on the spot fine for speeding. Shortly after we found that speeding was an impossibility as we were now in heavily wooded foothills ascending sharply into fairly high mountains.

Chapter Twelve

As ever, when arriving anywhere, evening was coming up fast and Lou, who was on home ground for the first time for thirty odd years, was as lost as we were. Colin, who was at the wheel, swore about the road, which by this time was more like a farm track. We passed a notice which we could hardly read in the gloom; at the time we thought it indicated detour but a little further on and up we found out what it meant.

We came to a chasm in the road with two planks across it. At the left hand side the road had rolled down the mountain and as I surveyed the sight I wondered how we would get out of such a tricky situation; I was sure we would have to back down the track, or camp where we were for the night. I tried to speak in as matter of fact voice as I could muster in order not to frighten the boys, when two things happened. Colin said, "Hold onto your hats, we're going forward," and at the same time Be fainted.

By the time I had Be sat up straight again in her seat we were across the chasm and found the road was on its way down the mountain.

We passed a solitary house and Lou went to ask directions. He found we were quite close to his village, and thankful we were to know it. We decided we could do without tea until we got to Lou's sister and Colin on a fairly good road now with no traffic got us there quickly.

Katica was alone in the house and as we expected there was a tearful reunion between brother and sister. She bustled round with a meal and despatched a grandchild to tell the clan to gather. Before we had finished the meal people began arriving, and after introductions were made they started on the serious business. Out came the Slivovice, someone began to sing and soon the house was bursting at the seams, as neighbours were drawn in by the music.

I said to Colin, "Mind what you are at with the booze. It will be stronger than anything you're used to."

He said to me the immortal words, "Don't worry Joan. I shall be O.K."

Everyone wanted to talk to us but couldn't, and some of the school children, who were taking English at school, on the strength of having a great Uncle in England, were too shy to attempt to speak, so everyone sat with shy smiles or big grins occasionally lifting their glases and saying, "Zivio", which being translated seems to mean "Carry on living".

One of Katica's sons took a special liking to George and although neither could speak directly to the other, they sat together and were lifting the glass to each other and shouting "Zivio" every five minutes. The young ones were soon having a job keeping thier eyes open, so Be and I decided to get to bed and leave the revellers to their bottles and songs. George decided he was ready too, and David and Colin opted to stay on for a while.

We were all in one enormous room with two big beds, two cots and two beds on the floor. Be and I took the beds on the floor, in case we needed to get up for the boys in the night, and left the beds for the men. Dave was the next to arrive and I said, "How's Colin?"

"Alright, while he's sitting down," he said, getting into bed.

Shortly after I was able to see how Colin was. As a newt and wiser after the event. He had never had a hangover before and he hasn't had one since. He said he needed to be sick so I looked for a suitable container, which was not easy. First there was no light except for my torch, and then in order to accommodate the extra beds, Katica had put all we would not need under the beds out of the way. I was crawling about under beds, moving, pushing and shoving, striving to reach a very large basin which I could see, while Colin was moaning, "Hurry up Joan," in funeral tones. I chose this moment to get a fit of the giggles. I suppose it was a release of the stresses of the day and maybe necessary on that account, but as I thrashed about under the bed George began to snore, I let out a shriek.

Be said "What is the matter Mum?" She switched on her torch, saw that my bed was empty and said, "Where are you?"

"Here, under the bed," I said, through my teeth, trying not to laugh and backpedalling to freedom, pulling the basin after me.

As I came out from under another snore made itself heard. I thought it was David, but not at all. It was my squiffy little friend who hadn't been able to wait for my mission to be completed.

Fortunately he was not taken ill in the night and a good night was had by all, including myself, although I had pains in my stomach from laughing in such a confined space and I had hit my head on the bedstead and felt as though I'd been through the mangle.

In the morning we were able to take stock of our surroundings. Martin and Barry, always used to water from a tap, were intrigued, to say the least when we had to wind the bucket down into the well, bringing up the coldest, clearest, brightest water we had ever had the pleasure of using.

Naturally the boys shrieked a bit about the face washing ceremony, and I could have shrieked myself to tell the truth, but it was all great fun, and also explained why in all the years Lou had been in the family, he had never used hot water for washing.

The farmyard was quite big, too big to cross late at night when one needed to pop to the toilet before bed. This primative toilet was no worry to Be and myself as we had been used to one for years, but this one carried a bonus. The way in was through a big barn which housed the horse, the cow, the farm implements, and once enthroned one could, and did have a conversation with the pig who loved company and would push his snout to a hole in the wood wall in order to have it scratched.

A large orchard was at the back of the barn, a most pleasant place where we could lie on a blanket under the cherry and plum trees and find total oblivion, if fancy lay in that direction.

All this was paradise to the boys who made big friends with all Katica's grandchildren and neighbouring children. The result was a gang of small boys charging about like a herd of buffalo, with no language barriers. As we watched, we came to the conclusion that a sort of psychic awareness was operating. All the children seemed to do the same thing together at exactly the same moment with no delay between the shouted word and the next action. It was quite uncanny, but neither language appeared to be of consequence.

The terrain was hilly around the village and at a further distance became mountainous. While Lou visited family and school friends, we had some good exploratory rambles around, but mostly enjoyed the elusive sun when it made an appearance.

There was a party each night in a different house with music, dancing and singing. We met the man who had taught Lou to play the guitar in his youth until Lou was able to take his place in the family band. The band travelled around every weekend to other villages, playing for weddings, but in the days before the war the wedding season was winter-time.

The rest of the year was always work, work and more work, in order to fill the barns and stores with food for themselves and fodder for the stock during the months when snow lay over the land, which could be a period of up of four months. During this time when they were shut in, or could travel with skis or snowshoes, the families would use the time to make the new bedding for the couples about to wed.

Every chicken, goose or duck used to feed the family during the winter months would make a further contribution in the way of its feathers, which would be kept aside until outside work was ended; then everyone would get busy cleaning and dressing the feathers ready for pillows, mattresses and quilts. The main rib was discarded and all else used.

All the women made their new clothes and did wonderful embroidery, mostly without glasses, as we noticed when we saw very old ladies making the finest lace, some of which they gave us as parting gifts.

Lou had a disappointment that he would not see his dead brother's son, Wilko; he was married and lived away from the home village, and had his job to go to and to make things more awkward he was due to take the family band away to a wedding engagement very early on Saturday morning. Be and I were up early in order to do the washing to date, so that we would have everything clean for the next leg of our trek.

With Katica's old copper boiler belching forth clouds of steam in the barn, Be and I were up to our elbows in soap suds in the yard, when a car pulled up in the road outside.

Be said, "Someone's about early today," and then around the corner of the house came a small procession, four young men, three carrying an instrument and one without. They nodded and smiled at us and set themselves up and proceeded to play. Music never sounded so good. Be and I rubbed in time to the music and became aware that a small crowd had come into the farmyard from outside, as well as Katica's son and his family from next door. After about twenty minutes they packed their instruments away, said their farewells, and drove off to the wedding. That memory is still very sharp for me, the dusty yard, steam billowing from the barn door, the squeal of the chain lowering and bringing up the bucket, the first batch of washing blowing on the line and Be and I each with a bowl on a trestle beside the well, and the music and voices soaring over all. It was wonderful.

As soon as the word went round that we were moving on we had a repeat performance of the presentations we had already experienced in Czechoslovakia. In vain to say we had no space, and with so many willing helpers all the excess got stowed away.

I recalled several times the awful chasm in the road that Colin had been able to negotiate and I thought we were being watched over by a strong power. Katica said we need not worry as once we were on the motorway all would be plain sailing.

I hoped she was to be proved right as we said our "goodbyes" and were waved away from the village by the usual groups.

Chapter Thirteen

With David driving the mini-bus set course for the motorway and we discussed the last few days as we went. We all agreed that it had not been easy for Katica to have her house invaded by so many foreign devils, at the same time as she had an emotional visit from her younger brother after an absense of such magnitude.

Our route led up and down the mountains for several miles until we joined the motorway west of Slavonski Brod. Here we stopped for a lunch break on a broad stretch of grass where we could watch the world go by and go by it did. Seemingly there were no speed limits, containers of one kind or another sped by so fast we were not able to read the names on the sides of the vehicles. George and I were just about to sit to our food when another facet of life on the motorway went past us in the shape of a herd of goats, and we conjectured on the fate of a herd of animals on the M1, not to mention the fate of the herdsman.

From where we sat, the road surface appeared nothing to write home about and we could see the joins in the tarmac as if the surface had been laid in squares; in fact, we were distinctly unhappy when an empty sand lorry tearing down the road made a series of metallic thumps as it went over the ridges. We knew we would not rise so high into the air as the lorry, because we were overloaded with all the stuff from the family in Czechoslavakia, some of which we had unloaded at Katica's only to have it replaced by the Yugoslavs.

While our four drivers studied the map, George and I cleared away the remains of the meal and discussed what we would have to eat when we stopped next time, checked that we had plenty of drinking-water for our all important tea, gathered up the boys who had been playing in an adjacent field, and were then ready for anything.

Travelling in the interior of the country we were surprised to find so many places geared up to the tourist's needs. Plenty of signs about in several languages, and a great number of campsites as we drove along. In 1971 there was a small trickle of people beginning to consider Yugoslavia as a holiday destination, but they had all been steered to the coastal areas, and although beautiful, there was still a lot of beauty and majestic scenery within the rest of the country.

All along the motorway we saw flowers hanging on trees and finally realised these were shrines where accidents had occurred. Where space was sufficient the vehicles were often left *in situ* as a warning to other travellers.

As we came closer to Belgrade we began to see people wearing more Eastern apparel. Two men talking on a street corner had baggy trousers to the knee and Turkish slippers with turned-up toes, which the boys thought very interesting.

Immediately beyond Belgrade, we decided to stop to eat on a very wide grass verge beside the road. We set up our stove and got a pan of soup going on one burner and the kettle on the other, and had a good look at the country around. There were level fields on both sides of the road with gently sloping hills beyond. We could see an ox cart working several fields away, and a little way past where we had chosen to stop were several piles of gravel just right for the two small boys to get to grips with. Right next to us was a field of maize six feet high which we would be grateful for before moving off.

When all was ready George called the gang together, soup bowls were filled, bread was passed round and we all found places to sit. We were nearly at the end of the meal when David said, "We've got company."

We looked up to find a long line of ox carts coming slowly towards us, with men and women riding and others walking beside the oxen, some faces expressionless, and one or two all smiles, especially the leading men.

"Dobar dan," he said. "Dobar dan," we all chorused in our best vernacular. He and Lou spoke a little and then the man with the leading ox cart spoke to David who looked somewhat startled. The only word we made out was 'radio' so David loked at Lou and asked, "What did he say?"

It transpired he wanted the radio which Dave had switched on while we ate

"Will you sell it?" said Lou.

"Of course I won't bloody sell it," was the reply.

Realising discretion to be the better part of valour, Lou ferreted about in the bus and brought out the Slivovice and a glass, pouring as he explained that the radio belonged to his friend and he was unwilling to sell and that we would need the radio for another week or so, but "Look out for us on the way back."

By now the cart people had moved to the piles of gravel and boulders to begin loading them, and their leader asked if the boys would like to ride in the cart; of course they would, thank you very much, so to their great glee they rode to the gravel heap in an empty cart and back on a full one. We took a picture and all parted company in a friendly manner, with me wondering how we would have managed if Lou had not shown himself to be a Yugoslav.

By the time the canteen staff had cleared away the dishes, having decided to do the washing up at our next stop the carts were almost out of sight, but we slipped smartly into the maize field, bundled into the bus and made off. I had really felt more than uncomfortable during our little exchange.

However, we soon had cause for a smile; a few miles on, making for Valdo's little town near the Rumanian border, we caught up with an old chap biking home from the field with his hoe, carried not along the length of the bike but across it, tied to the frame under the saddle. He took up as much space on the motorway as a continental freight carrier and we found it impossible to pass him and followed behind him for a couple of miles before he turned off the road, leaving us free passage.

Bowling along with Be at the wheel we came to a diversion marker and found we had exchanged the tarmac for a sandy track which meandered in a lackadaisical manner across bumpy ground. We seemed to be descending slightly through boulders and scrub when we rounded a bend and saw the terrain spread out before us. The bushes became more sparse and the track led down to a small stream with a bridge across it. Coming down toward the bridge on the other side of the stream was a little old lady driving two large pigs.

We continued to drive slowly down toward the bridge, thinking the woman must have seen us, then as we approached the bridge from our side she caught sight of us. She pulled her long black skirts up to her knees and leapt into the air, laying about the pigs furiously to turn them from our path. It was such a ludicrously athletic sight we could hardly believe we had seen it happen and we fell about laughing, and when we looked back she was still rounding her pigs up and trying to get them onto the bridge.

During the miles from the diversion we had not seen another vehicle and we had begun to question if we had somehow gone off the straight and narrow, when the track levelled out and we came again onto a tarmac road. As it turned out there had been a landslip and that part of the motorway had disappeared during the early autumn rains with which the country had welcomed us.

A little further on we came to a garage and we called in for petrol. Several cars were in the forecourt and we were on the verge of driving off when George said, "Look there's Vlado," and sure enough there he was with his wife and children, waiting as he had done the day before the arrival of his dad and friends.

We went through the, 'one on each cheek and one in the middle' exercise again, quite used to it by now, and had a sort of celebration there in the garage forecourt to the interest of the customers and staff alike, then piled into the bus, but this time Lou rode with Vlado and his family and we brought up the rear.

We drove through a gorge with high cliffs on each side and heavy metal mesh erected to catch the falling rocks as explained in the many signs we passed, feeling thankful to have finally come to a stop for the next few days. Once again we had arrived after dark.

We drove into the centre of the little town and pulled up outside a small block of flats with parking spaces. Vlado had reserved one for us for the few days we were to be there. We each took a case, a bag or bundle and followed the family up the stairs, thinking of baths, showers and washing-machines.

Chapter Fourteen

As ever, out came the bottle and all the men settled down together. Be and I freshened up the boys and ourselves and began to prepare for the wash-day in the morning.

Vlado and his family had moved to their friend's flat along the balcony, so we had plenty of space; I have to say that at the time I had not realised the generosity of such a gesture, both on the part of the family and on that of the friends.

While all this was being explained to us, Jovanka was producing some good smells from the kitchen and we began to anticipate our dinner with interest.

When the call came, we had both a shock and a suprise, for filling a large meat platter was a suckling pig. It looked so scrumptious it could have been varnished, and with it we had boiled potatoes, mushrooms and salad. Jovanka and her family did not eat with us, but took on the role of waiters and served the honoured guests, who were horribly embarrassed at the situation. None the less, we partook with great relish and ended up with greasy chins to a man.

My family needed an early night, so we left Lou to get to know his son and his family better, this being his first meeting with his grandson and grandaughter and also his daughter-in-law.

The next morning Jovanka put her washing machine at our disposal, but in the end sent us all out to look at the town with Vlado. This excursion developed into a progress as the word seemed to have gone round that the Engleski were about and everywhere we went, people were watching us. We passed the hotel and the windows were filled with folk staring at us. We stopped at the kiosk in the square to buy cards and stamps, and half the town were buying cards.

One very nice thing was that from time to time someone would come up to speak to Lou, obviously paying great deference to the father of Vlado, himself a man of standing in the town by reason of the job he was doing. It was pleasant to see such respect given to the older people in view of the fact that respect for anyone is practically nil in our own country nowadays.

The weather by now was very cold, with lots of rain thrown in. I was beginning to wonder if George was in line for another of his illnesses; we had left home with plenty of tablets, but he had already made inroads into those so we kept our fingers crossed that all would go well from now on.

He was enjoying the holiday in spite of two little 'turns' he had already suffered, in fact, had we wished to travel by air, our doctor would have strongly advised against George taking part at all. So, always an optimist, he took in all the sights and sounds as he went along and particularly loved the magnificent scenery and the wonderful air at the top of every mountain, which then made breathing so much easier for him. Accordingly he avoided extremes of cold and wet and ate and slept well.

Thinking of the weather normally experienced in Jugoslavia, I had brought only one cardigan with me, and getting it dried after washing it had been awkward, to say the least, so I decided I ought to buy another in the town while there. Vlado said that I should wait until Jovanka was with us as she worked in the only department store in town, so this we did.

On arriving back at the house from our tour of the town, we were met by an embarrassed Jovanka who spoke urgently to Vlado, who then spoke urgently to Lou, who made deprecatory gestures to Jovanka, whose face was changing colour from white to red at a great rate. Agitated, and upset as she was, we followed her into the bathroom which housed the washing-machine, where she threw out a hand dramatically toward the washer. Peering inside we saw an unsavory looking mess in pea-green and some pea-green articles in a bowl beside it. It began to emerge that, by mistake, a shirt of Lou's had gone in with the whites and that, as a consequence, everyone had undies in the colour of the month, pea-green no less. Poor Jovanka, she had wanted everything to be right for her father-in-law and his English 'family'. She was mortified so we all gave her a cuddle and assured her, through Lou, that at last our dreams had come true and we all had matching undies in PEA-GREEN.

When we went to the store the next day to buy my cardigan I had three assistants, plus Jovanka. They measured me around and also my sleeve length and as we left the counter with the rest of the gang, we could hear giggles and shrieks as Jovanka told a long tale. Since then we have often asked her, "What is the colour of the month?" over the phone and it is now a family joke both here and there.

Jovanka's mum and dad lived twenty miles away on the banks of the Danube. Most of the residents were fisherfolk and we had been invited for the main meal of the day. They had a lovely one-storied house right on the edge of the river, set in a large garden and to get to it you walked under a canopy of vines with luscious grapes almost brushing your face as you walked.

A long trestle table had been set up, places laid and an assortment of seating alongside. The usual bottles were produced to go with the glasses already in evidence and Vlado's family all began to tell the grandparents of my odd way of going on. By this time I left the others to tell the tale, as I had had such a spate of embarrassment previously when everyone began to explain me to everyone else, but these two old people made no bones about it.

They lifted their glasss to me and said, "Zivio" from time to time and I responded with a rumbustrious, "Zivio" so they would understand I was really enjoying myself. I was too; their garden was pleasant with a large number of oleanders, plenty of geraniums and fuchias and naturally the ubiquitous grape. There was no pattern scheme or theme to any of the gardens we saw, everything just grew as the seed from the previous year fell and there were no lawns or hard paths anywhere.

I imagine the gardens look much as the old cottage gardens looked in England pre 1914, although I saw no hollyhocks, pinks or sweet williams, but there were some roses and everyone had a straggly old type lavender bush.

When mealtime drew near Jovanka laid the outside table under the vine pergola and when called to the table we wasted no time at all to sit down. I noticed Vlado and all his family sat with us and Jovanka's mum and dad did the honours.

First came the inevitable soup tureen and bread platter and our host served Lou first and then came to me. "Riba," he said with a smile and pointed to the Danube. I smiled and said, "lovely," and took a mouthful. I froze where I sat. Fish soup no less. I thought, "You'd pay the earth for fish soup in a good restaurant," that is, if you wanted fish soup. I caught George's eye across the table; he gave an almost imperceptible shake of his head at the precise moment that Martin and Barry said, "I don't like it mum."

Hastily Be said to Lou, "Please tell them that the boys won't have their soup", only to hear Colin mutter, "Nor will I thanks," and David said, "I'm the same." So in order to save our group's collective face, it was left to Be and myself to not only finish up what was already in our dishes, but to have seconds as well; we performed manfully, or womanfully in this case, and we were rewarded twice for our trouble, first we saw the smile return to the faces which had gone blank at the sight of the guests who were not eating, and then again when the next course arrived. Yes, it was more "Riba", but what a fish it turned out to be.

We had never tasted anything like it before or since. It was magnificent. There were three large dishes, each a different fish and each cooked in a different way. All the backsliders tucked in and a good time was had by all, but fish soup has gone down in the archives, and when Colin is with us we unfailingly recall it.

After the meal Lou translated for our host, who thought the boys would like to go out in the boat; of course they could not get there soon enough, so while Jovanka and her daughter helped our hostess clear away and wash the dishes, we made our way down to the jetty, leaving Vlado, George, David, Colin and Lou to a bottle-tipping session.

The day had been sunny and fairly warm, and I looked forward to the river trip and in the event it was a very interesting exercise. Our host pulled for the further shore; about halfway across we could see bushes standing out of the water, and as soon as we got among them he stopped rowing, said a few words and pointed downwards.

What a sight met our eyes. Through the crystal clear water we were looking straight down on a village far below. There was the main street with the houses and gardens, some had a wooden seat still in place; there was a broken farm cart at the side of one house, and a little way along the village street another road crossed it at right-angles. The sun, through the water, dappled the buildings and a slight current set the grasses and bushes in the gardens below into a lazy motion.

The boys were enchanted and wanted to know why the houses were drowned, and what happened to all the people? Our guide pulled a couple of times on the oars in order for us to see farther along the street and we found ourselves above the church; the top of the tower was about four feet below us and I wondered if the bell was ever set in motion by the current. I found the sight a sad one; people had been married and buried and prayed over from that church, and not for the first time during that holiday, I badly wished I could have a proper conversation with the people we met. I felt I would have liked to hear more about the flooding of the area and how the rehousing had been dealt with by their system.

We heard a faint hooter in the distance and Jovanka's dad pointed to the further shore. "Roumania," he said, and as we looked a heavy locomotive travelled sluggishly across the landscape on the far side. We were later told that it is quite common for the locals to cross into Roumania for shopping trips; and had we been in the area for longer we would have asked to go, but our time was getting short and our departure was imminent.

We took leave of Vlado and the family, with him saying he would be seeing us in England before too long, but with two young ones to consider, it was to be twenty-odd years before they saw England in 1985. In fact, we had made another trip to Lou's home village in 1982, and saw them all again there.

We reflected on all we had seen and done while in Vlado's town and as we bowled along on the motorway Martin wanted to know why "That old lady jumped into the air," and Barry wondered why all those people's houses "got drowned," and in no time at all it was time to camp for the night.

We had travelled north-west for some miles passing Belgrade on our left, then beyond Slavonski Brod, where we had joined the big road coming from Katica's.

Shortly after we found a very wide verge bordering a maize field and a house nearby. Lou took the water carrier and asked permission to stay the night which was given at once as was the water, then George and I got into our stride preparing the meal.

We had taken plenty of tinned food and dried soups, which had proved a blessing on the days when the weather had been so cold. We had plenty of fresh baked bread and a large selection of salami to choose from, thanks to the generosity of family and friends. Added to this we had great bags of peaches and plums, so the canteen duties were not too onerous.

Suddenly the stillness was broken by sirens and down the motorway at a very fast speed came a motorcade of black official-looking limousines. We counted seven cars and as many motorbikes and a man in a passing car stuck his head out of his window, pointed his thumb and shouted, "Kruschev" and disappeared into the evening gloom. We came to the conclusion it was a Russian delegation, in the country to see President Tito.

We cleared away the meal things and got ready for bed hoping for a better day with some sun.

We were not to have solar heating the next day either; the morning was drizzly and nippy, so we lost no time in folding our tents and stealing away, being waved off by the occupants of the nearby house who had evidently watched us packing up.

Our drivers had been studying the routes and as it was still the tourist season, decided to miss roads used by coastal traffic, which meant coming off the motorway before Zagreb and travelling across country to Varazdin, where we could take a good road on to Maribor and across the border into Austria.

An uneventful journey brought us to Maribor, with the weather not on our side at all, so there was no incentive to get out of the mini-bus to look about, and we pressed on.

Arriving at the crossing point, we all got out to find toilets and there was a sign which we followed over a small bridge, and found we had crossed the frontier to get to the toilets before we crossed in the mini-bus. I hope the system has been changed now, in view of the volume of traffic these days.

Fairly high mountains had been around us for some time but the rain and mist obscured the summits and the grandeur of the scenery was not apparent, but the pretty Austrian houses with geraniums and petunias tumbling from every balcony were a joy to see, rain or not. Every village was so clean, not a speck of litter to be seen, as if some giant hand had been along with a brush and smartened everything up only a minute before.

Through Klagenfurt it was decided to stop at the next camping site, the sign for which appeared on the way to Villach.

We turned off the road, up a rising path between sloping grass meadows clinging to the sides of the mountains, and another sign sent us sharp right into an empty car park. As the engine died another sound came to us.

Above the lashing rain a mountain torrent was crashing its exuberant way over rocks very near us, although we were unable to see it. Telling the others to stay put, Be and I got out to see if there was anyone about. There was a camper van in a corner, but no sign of life, although a water-sodden banner limply declaimed "Up the Aussies." to anyone who cared to read it.

A small range of buildings showed itself and turned out to be a shop-cum-cafe, plus washrooms. Lights were in the cafe and in the rooms above, and as we were trying to decide whether to enter the cafe or go to the side door, the owner appeared.

We asked if we could stay the night, he asked us where we came from. I said England and he replied that he knew London. By now we were inside the shop and he explained that the season was at an end and that they were closing for winter, but one night would be fine. We wrote our details in his book and he said, "There are some children also?" We nodded and he said, "Very bad weather for the young," and then, as an after thought, he said, "We have very much hot water for baths and tea-making. No charge. You are very happy to use it."

I thanked him very much for his kindness and said we would see him later on and he said that we were to go in and ask for any help we may need.

Back at the van Colin said, "George is not too good Joan," and I could see he was not quite the thing.

I decided to make a bed for him in the van with Lou for that night so that whatever the weather did, he would be at least dry.

The rest of the gang were struggling to erect the tent, unsuccessfully as it happened, so telling George to stay in the warm I went out to lend a hand. By now it was dim and murky and through the gloom a light was coming across the car park. It was our host in waterproofs and wellies to tell us to drive the bus to the cafe door, unload all our gear and and to "feel at home and not mess with the tent on such a night." He stopped all our thanks with, "All will be good. You are English."

No tent was ever put away so fast and we were soon inside. We moved tables and chairs to put all our sleeping-bags and sleeping gear down on the floor, and it made us all laugh to see this row of assorted lilos and foam mattresses in line against the wall. Everyone did a job and in no time at all we were fed, and very comfortable.

The owner came in to see if we were all O.K. and wanted to know what time we wanted to leave. I said we were anxious to make an early start, and nearly fell over when he said, "Pay me tonight and go when you wish."

Looking at the bottles on the shelves and all the tins, jars and packets I thought he must be nuts, but he must have read my thoughts, for he said, "That is good, don't worry." Thereupon, I paid him, he hoped we would sleep well, wished us a pleasant journey home, and was gone.

We had anything but a good night, all of us were ill, except (guess who) George, who lay in bed laughing at the rest as we made innumerable visits to the toilet or the sink, whichever we could reach first.

By morning we felt a bit washed out but made breakfast of an assortment of remains of packets, making space for a new batch of shopping at the next place we came to.

Chapter Fifteen

Before leaving the campsite we went to look at the mountain stream which had greeted us so noisily the previous evening. Not so lively this morning as the rain had ceased during the night. The summits were hidden behind a slight mist, although there was a promise of better things to come, and after leaving a bottle of Evka's wine on the counter with a note of thanks in my fractured German, together with Lou's name and address, we drove out and on to the main road. Lou had Christmas cards for five years after.

It has to be said that some of us were getting restless for home; Lou could not wait to get home to his birds and the boys who had been so well behaved were beginning to ask, "How much further grandad?" Colin harnessed their interest by saying we would be on the top of one of those mountains before long, and at intervals their question changed to, "When shall we get to the top of the mountain Colin?"

As a child, Colin had previously spent two holidays in Austria and retained fond memories of the country and its people and said he would love to go over the ground again. If we did this it would entail going up and over the Grosser Glockner. We all thought that it would be a great idea to see Austria's highest mountain, conveniently forgetting our hair-raising experience on the outward journey to Katica's village.

We all did our own jobs; George and I seeing to the canteen at our stops, and the driving team sorting out their petrol money, distances and times, hoping that for once we could arrive in daylight. At the first opportunity Be and I replenished our stocks of necessities and bought lovely hot new bread. We were all feeling much better and ready to face anything that might turn up.

We bowled along in sunshine towards Colin's dream, not expecting any shocks, but one was lying in wait at the toll-gate at the foot of the mountain road. The cost was more than we expected, when it is not more, but we had to go forward, so we took half from the petrol pool and the rest from the canteen money and were on our way up.

The ascent was magical, all of us were quiet, lost in the beauty and grandeur of it all. There had been a mad scramble for sunglasses to counteract the glare of sun on snow, the first time we had all needed them; then further on we scrambled to get our woollies as the temperature dropped.

Finally at the top, Colin stopped the bus and we all got out, struggling into our jackets and shivering in the thin air. We found we were standing on a small plateau with the peaks of all the other mountains slightly below us and spreading out for miles and miles around.

George loved it. He said fresh air had got into the nooks and crannies in his lungs he never knew he had and he was sorry when the cold and old Father Time drove us back into the vehicle.

Our enjoyment continued all the way down the other side with a magnificent spectacle spread before us and sometimes a small cluster of pretty houses in a fold in the mountains.

For once I was sitting in the front beside Colin who drove. Mostly I had sat at the back, so I could quickly get whatever was wanted from the conglomeration of tackle we had accumulated on our travels. Only Be or I were able to ferret about in the more or less correct spot for the item required.

As we covered the ground I became aware things were not quite the ticket. I leaned across and asked, "All right Col?"

He said from the side of his mouth, "Not really. Brakes have gone I think."

Always cool in a crisis, no matter how I might go to pot after it, I said in my usual voice, "If you have poor tools mate, you have to do specially good work."

He smiled a thin smile as we went into another bend in the road and incredibly, the road before us began to rise, and at the side nearest the mountain there was a wide grass verge with no obstructions. He steered us into it and switched off.

We had only a small distance to travel before the road levelled out and we were into the town along the lakeshore, but because time was short to begin with, and more was wasted investigating the brakes business the chance for Colin to see the nearby places he had once know was lost, and as soon as the bus was ready for the road we were off again.

Looking for a site to lay our heads, we found a most picturesque monastery set in a large meadow with trees and flowering shrubs around. We rubbed our hands with glee, but self-congratulation was not in order the following morning. The monastery bell had tolled all through the night, every quarter of an hour, and we could sympathise with Tom after his losing bout with Jerry when he cracks and shatters to bits. We could have done the same.

From then on it was all systems 'go' for home and our driving team fixed a rota so we made no more stops to Calais. We replenished our stocks of bread, milk and eggs and took off without meeting any further problems.

Without the mountains the world seemed spacious, but uninteresting. The boys took naps, and we played Snap. Our drivers changed and slept and it seemed in no time at all we were at a site outside Calais waiting, for our early crossing next day.

Our drivers had had one or two frights driving through France, where the motto seems to be 'All for one,' Alexandre Dumas had never envisaged the motor age, it was clear, although three musketeers on one motor bike was a common sight.

The campsite at Calais was on the cliff top and not exactly a place for tents, although there were a large number of them, but it was a constant battle to stop anything not weighted down from blowing out to sea.

We were very lucky with our crossing, the sea was calm and the sun shone and we all enjoyed the unaccustomed motion after three weeks solidly on the road.

As soon as we were released from customs at Dover, I rang home to tell the aunts and uncle that we were on our way and it was arranged that they would be ready to go home as we arrived, and without more ado we set off for the home base at a cracking pace.

We had all had a great experience; had enjoyed our swift peep behind the Iron Curtain; had faces put to names of people we had known of for twenty years, but had never seen. I was more than thankful that George had made it home safely and with two tablets to spare, and friendships had been forged that I hoped would last for my grandsons' lifetimes, as well as my own. As I write, years after the events, there is still a two-way link between our two countries, resulting in grand reunions from time to time.

Our arrival home created pandemonium, the dogs rushed about, the parrot alternated between "Bye-bye" and "Hello grandma." Our cases went in, the caretaking team's cases came out; after hellos there were goodbyes and the crowd began to thin out.

We loaded up the relatives and Lou took them home, Be and Dave rounded up the boys and went to their place, Colin, who was undoubtably hero of the expedition, when you think of the hairy bits, went off to raid his mum's cake tin, and George and I sat among the debris of cases, boxes, and carrier-bags, completely sold out.

"Stay where you are," he said, "I'll put the kettle on."